# KITTY
## STUFF

# KITTY
# STUFF

FROM NAILS TO TAIL —

A CONCISE, INFORMATIONAL BABY BOOK

FOR TODAY'S BUSY KITTY "PARENTS"

Jodi Alessandrini & Kathy Kinser

Illustrations by Diane M. Cape

Pallachip Publishing, Springfield, Illinois

Pallachip Publishing
37 Oakmont Drive
Springfield, IL 62704

Copyright ©2002 by Jodi Alessandrini and Kathy Kinser
Printed in the United States of America by Walsworth Publishing Company, Marceline, Missouri

Illustrations by Diane M. Cape; Cover Design by Diane M. Cape and Jodi Alessandrini
Veterinary Sources: Louis Brad, DVM;  Franklin A. Coble, DVM;  Janet L. Hill, DVM; Gregory B. Hurst, DVM; Paul McGowan, DVM; Gregory S. Riffell, DVM; Stacey A. Conner-Riffell, DVM.

**Note:** Kitty Stuff is not meant to be a complete guide to cat care.  The content is accurate to the best of the authors' knowledge.  The book should be used as a general guide.  Feline health care requires the services of a veterinarian.  The authors, Pallachip Publishing, or their agents cannot guarantee the results of any of the recommendations in Kitty Stuff.  The authors, Pallachip Publishing, and their agents associated with Kitty Stuff disclaim any liability from the use of any information in Kitty Stuff or any loss or damage caused, or alleged to be caused, directly or indirectly, by the information contained in this book.

ISBN 0-9647465-1-4

10 9 8 7 6 5 4 3 2 1

First Printing - 2002
Library of Congress Cataloging-in-Publication Data available upon request
This book is available at quantity discount for 14 or more books.
For information, call (217)546-4825
Visit our home page at http://www.kitnpupstuff.com

## TO SOME REAL PUSSY CATS!

To Dale and Miss Flori, whose "kitty stuff" inspired us to write this book. Thanks for shredding all the parts you didn't like.

And to Helen for inspiring Diane to create such adorable drawings.

And to Gizmo, Mariah, Turbo, Ajax, Tigger, Spunky, Wayne, Garth, Kumu, Molson, Boo Kitty, Ripper, Friday, Clyde, Oscar, Crazy, Mattie, Jenny, OJ, Puck, Cassandra, Tabitha, Frazzle, Alice D., Sophie, Cheech, Maimie, Tom, Whitey, Bear, Stripes, Dickens, Daisy, Phantom and Gatsby for all the very lovely memories included in our book. We love and cherish you all!

We also dedicate this book to all the men and women who volunteer their time in animal shelters throughout the world.

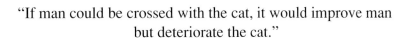

DALE
"CHIEF SHREDDER"

MISS FLORI
"ROVING SHREDDER"

"If man could be crossed with the cat, it would improve man
but deteriorate the cat."

Mark Twain

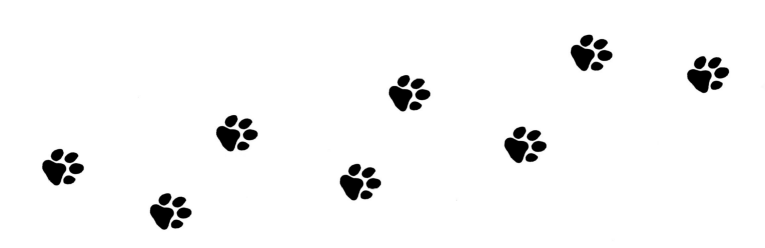

# SPECIAL THANKS

*To our veterinarian friends, for making us appear smarter than we are*

**Louis Brad,** DVM, is a 1986 graduate of the University of Illinois, College of Veterinary Medicine. He has practiced in Illinois, North Carolina and presently owns the Gunbarrel Veterinary Clinic in Boulder, Colorado. His prior work with the Southern Illinois Humane Society influenced his philosophy about the role of animals in our lives. Wayne and Garth, his two rescued office cats, benefit from his philosophy as do all animals in his care. Marriage to Candy Sayles, also a  veterinarian, gave Kumu, his house cat, two more feline companions, Molson and Boo Kitty. They all share their home with three dogs, Ren, Tonka and Hozer.

**Franklin A. Coble,** DVM, is a 1970 graduate of the University of Illinois, College of Veterinary Medicine. He owns and operates Coble Animal Hospital in Springfield, Illinois which was established by his father, J. Porter Coble, DVM. His two black Labrador dogs, Lady and Puppy, accompany him to work everyday.

**Janet L. Hill**, DVM, is a 1992 graduate of the University of Missouri at Columbia. Upon graduation, she began practice in Boonville, Missouri. She is now a practice owner at West Lake Animal Hospital in Springfield, Illinois. She resides in Springfield with her husband, Jeff, their sons, Taylor and Drew, a mutt named Buddy, and two cats, Crazy (a stray aptly named by her son, Taylor) and Mattie. Mattie showed up at her front door one day and never left.

**Gregory B. Hurst**, DVM, is a 1984 graduate of the University of Illinois, College of Veterinary Medicine. He returned to his hometown of Springfield, Illinois to open his practice. He and his wife, Ann, have two children, Chip and Hilary. Their family pets are a West Highland white terrier named Dolly and a long-haired calico cat named Jenny.

**Paul McGowan**, DVM, is a 1986 graduate of the University of Illinois, College of Veterinary Medicine. He practices now in Chatham, Illinois at The Village Veterinarian. He and his wife, Jane Morris, DVM, live with a Corgi, Emma, and two cats, OJ and Puck.

**Gregory S. Riffell**, DVM, and **Stacey A. Conner-Riffell**, DVM, are graduates of Oklahoma State University, College of Veterinary Medicine. They practice at Natomas Animal Medical Center in Sacramento, California, where Greg is the managing veterinarian. They are the parents of a son, Ethan. The remainder of their family includes a black lab mix named Lizzie, a Walker Coonhound named Shelby and two very happy cats, Cassandra and Tabitha.

*To our illustrator friend, for giving life to our text*

**Diane M. Cape** lives with canines, Tyler and Darby, and husband, Chuck Cali. She is a graduate of Illinois State University, and has been an illustrator for more than twenty years. Previously, they all had the privilege of being owned by a lovely orange cat named Helen.

**To our accounting friend, for keeping us in the black**

**Joseph A. Alessandrini** is a certified public accountant and a partner in the midwest regional CPA firm of Kerber, Eck and Braeckel LLP.

**To our computer and typesetter friend, for making us look terrific**

**Becky McVay** is a graphic artist who applied striking color to the drawings in <u>Kitty Stuff</u>. Becky attended Southern Illinois University at Carbondale and Sangamon State University at Springfield (now University of Illinois at Springfield,) with a major in Communications. Her background includes illustration, photography, and computer-enhanced images. Becky and her children share the two family cats, Maimie and Bear and two dog pals, Lily and Otto. Becky has been employed as a graphic artist for over twenty-five years, is currently illustrating a children's book and exhibits her original fine art in downstate Illinois.

**To our editing friends, for making us appear literate**

**Jeri Heminghous** is the Director of Educational and Specialty Sales for Global Software Publishing, North America, Inc. She lives in Colorado with husband, Mark, and their cats, lady-like Mariah, Turbo, who lives up to his name, and Ajax, the kitten warrior. Their fourth cat, Gizmo died recently at the age of sixteen. During his lifetime he lived in four different states and adjusted well to each move. He was a very noble and wise Siamese cat.

**Linda Kopecky** was a college English teacher for many years before a recent move to the Illinois State Board of Education.

**Janet Reinhart** and husband Dan, formerly of Springfield, Illinois, have been transplanted to St. Louis along with three cats — Dickens, Daisy, and Phantom.

**To our other friends and family, for their unwavering support**

**Julie Costa** lives with her husband, Mario, their two cats, Tigger and Spunky, and their dog, Sophie. Julie is a real cat and dog lover. Since moving to the country, she has rescued and found homes for three cats and one dog.

**Pat Kendall**, affectionately known as The Fishlady®, is the author of <u>The Fishlady's® Cookbook</u>. Pat and her husband, Butch, share their household with two lively dachshunds, PeeNut and Curley. Their third dachshund, thirteen year old Pee Wee, died recently. Pat has placed pictures and cherished memories of PeeWee in <u>Puppy Stuff</u> which helps fill the empty space in her heart.

**David E. Kinser** is a retired Springfield ophthalmologist. As Kathy's husband, he was a supportive voice throughout the creation of <u>Kitty Stuff</u>.

**Cheryl White** and husband, Neville, were adopted by Stripes, a pregnant cat who gave and received love for twenty plus years before her recent death. Presently, Cheryl and her husband dote on Libby, a black toy poodle.

**To our readers, for buying our book and keeping us out of debt —**
**A very special thank you to all!**

# CONTENTS

## PAWS to consider

## POEMS

## MY INFORMATION

## MY PHOTOS

# INTRODUCTION

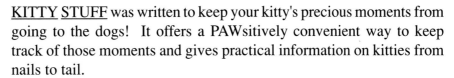

KITTY STUFF was written to keep your kitty's precious moments from going to the dogs! It offers a PAWsitively convenient way to keep track of those moments and gives practical information on kitties from nails to tail.

The "PURRsonals" pages provide space for recording, in chronological order, kitty's progress, special events, best moments, and medical records. In addition, there are ample spaces for mounting those fabulous fotos of your fetching feline.

The "PAWS to consider" sections, reviewed by several veterinarians, succinctly cover a wide variety of kitty care topics. Kitty related poetry is sprinkled throughout the book for a lighthearted view of your kitten from yet another perspective. Plus, tear-out cat-sitter/kennel cards are included for your convenience.

KITTY STUFF is based on knowledge the authors have gained from their experiences with their cats. It is easy to read, with information uniquely presented from your kitten's point of view. The book was created to capture the delights of kittenhood and beyond, and to foster a bond between you and your kitten.

From two cat lovers to another, best wishes for enjoying all the "kitty stuff" your kitten will provide.

Who seldom greets me at the door?
But saunters in across the floor.

Whose purring says, "I'm glad you're here!
I need a scratch behind my ear."

Who stares at me each time I dine?
Then tries to sip some of my wine.

Who sits with me to watch t.v.?
Then falls asleep upon my knee.

Who thinks <u>my</u> sleeping is a bore?
And taps my face if I should snore.

Who loves me when I look a mess?
Whose paw gives me a soft caress?

Who likes a hug and gentle squeeze?
Who's at its best, when it is pleased?

**MY KITTY!**

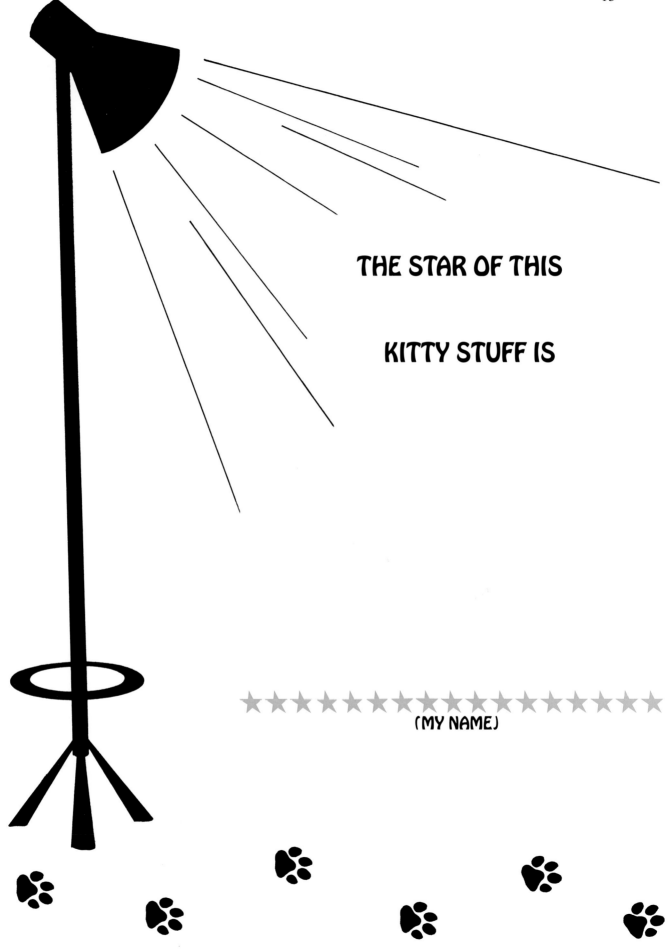

THE STAR OF THIS

KITTY STUFF IS

★★★★★★★★★★★★★★★★★★★

(MY NAME)

# THE COMMITMENT

The commitment you make when you bring home a pet,
Is a **PROMISE** to care for it.  **NEVER FORGET** . . .

Every year there are too many cats put to sleep,
All because of a promise their owners won't keep.

So honor your promise, secure kitty's fate.
By keeping vet visits and shots up to date.

Just neuter or spay.  There is no need to mate.
This planet can't handle the feline birth rate.

Your cat has a right to be safe and secure
With love that a nurturing home can ensure!

It is really quite smart to keep kitty inside
'Cause a car and a kitty should never collide!

Though safety is fine, it is not quite enough.
Include a nametag with your new kitty's stuff!

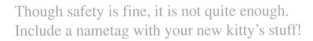

When kitty grows into a well-behaved pet,
It's just one of many rewards you will get.

Like friend and companion, a cat that is true,
Good natured, and happy; a credit to **YOU**!

 AWS to consider

YOUR COMMITMENT. When you adopt me, think of me as a furry toddler who no longer has the security of its mother or littermates. I will not understand the human language just as you may not understand my cat language. I will have traits you find adorable and others that are annoying. It is your job to enhance the adorable and correct the annoying. However, bear in mind that, like you, I will never be perfect!

As my cat "parent", please promise to do the following:

- Love me as a member of the family.
- Nourish me with nutritionally complete feline food.
- Provide me with quality health care.
- Exercise me to stimulate me mentally and physically.
- Train me with patience and kindness.
- Never abandon me.
- Respect me and let me live and die with dignity.

**TABBY TIPS**
Egyptians raised us to god-like stature. In fact, causing harm to a cat was punishable by death.

If you fulfill these promises, I will:

- bond with you
- learn to trust you
- try to obey, if I understand
- be a comfort and a faithful friend
- do my best to maintain a mouse-free environment

Due to our highly adaptable nature, self-sufficiency, and low maintenance, cats have surpassed the dog as the number one household pet in the United States. We are taken to nursing homes to increase smiles in the elderly, are greeters at local businesses, and are therapy for patients in health care facilities.

I know you have given a great deal of thought to obtaining me. I am a trusting pet who depends on your good judgement for my care. I am not disposable. Realistically, you can expect me to live for ten to eighteen years or more. I will consume some of your time, energy, and financial resources. I must be fed, groomed, trained, socialized, and taken to the veterinarian as needed. I will require love, attention, and exercise daily.

If at any time, you decide that your expectations about cat ownership were unrealistic or that you acquired me on impulse, please do not abandon me, for I cannot protect myself. Unless I was trained to hunt by my mother, I cannot provide food for myself. Please do the right thing! Return me to my original owner or find a loving home for me. Often bulletin boards at veterinary clinics have names of people seeking my type or breed. You could take me to a no-kill shelter with a donation to cover my costs until my new home is found. Remember, I trust you as my caregiver.

PETiculars

**TABBY TIPS**
Most Popular Cat Names:
Fluffy       Tiger
Charlie      Smokey
Missy        Muffin
Sammy        Patches
Tigger       Kitty

_____
MY NAME

My owner chose this name because _____

_____

## PAWS to consider

> **MY NAME.** What's in a name? Plenty! Two syllable words are easiest for me to understand. When I respond to my name, give me a treat and some caresses. Of course, as a cat, I may decide the appropriate time to respond. Once you have chosen my name, be consistent. Avoid confusing me by using other names or terms of endearment. Strengthen the bond between us by talking often to me using my name.

My breed _____

My distinctive markings _____

My eye color _____

Date of birth _____ I am a male/female (circle one)

My place of birth _____ (if known)

My weight at birth _____ (if known)  My present weight _____

Mom's Name _____ (if known)

Dad's Name _____ (if known)

My new people "parent(s)" name(s) _____

My new home address _____

My age upon arriving at my new home _____

I was adopted from _____

My "parent(s)" chose me because _____

_____

18

## PAWS to consider

**SELECTING A VETERINARIAN.** Seek recommendations, and then make an appointment with the veterinarian of your choice. During the visit, consider the following:

- Does the veterinarian take time to answer your questions and explain procedures and options in an understandable way?
- Is he/she familiar with my breed and my peculiarities?
- Does he/she seem interested in keeping up with new procedures and technologies?
- Does he/she handle me gently?
- Does he/she practice preventive medicine?
- Is the facility close and available in case I have an emergency? Is an alternative, such as an emergency medical center, available for times when the veterinary facility cannot provide services?
- Is the veterinary facility clean?

**VETERINARY VISITS.** Take me to my veterinarian or emergency clinic when I have any of the following problems:

- abnormal bowel movements
- abscesses
- a cold
- any injuries
- bloating
- blood in the stool or urine
- bloody nose
- broken bones
- burns
- choking or difficulty breathing
- constant drooling or bad breath
- constant head shaking
- difficulty or inability to control urination
- excessive discharge from my nose or eyes
- excessive hair loss or mange
- fever
- foul odor from my ears
- frostbite
- heatstroke
- jaundice
- lack of energy

- lack of interest in water or excessive thirst
- lameness or difficulty standing
- loss of consciousness
- lumps on or under my skin
- persistent coughing
- personality changes
- poisoning
- presence of parasites
- seizures
- shock (unresponsive pupils or complete immobility)
- skin rashes
- sores in my mouth
- sprains
- sudden loss of appetite
- sudden weight loss or gain
- tenderness or pain when touched
- vomiting blood or excessive vomiting
- wounds

**KITTENS AND CATS NEED PROFESSIONAL VETERINARY CARE!**

# PAWS to consider

## MY VETERINARIAN

Name _____

Address _____

_____

Phone _____

**The following is a suggested schedule of inoculations and tests. For specific information, consult my veterinarian.**

| | |
|---|---|
| 7 - 9 weeks: | Test for feline leukemia virus and feline AIDS virus. During the first year, bring a fecal sample each time we visit my veterinarian in order to test for intestinal parasites. Then continue yearly or as needed. |
| | VACCINATIONS: |
| 9 weeks: | FeLV (Leukemia virus)<br>1st FVRCP<br>    (Viral rhinotracheitis-calcivirus-panleukopenia) |
| 12 weeks: | FeLV booster (Leukemia virus)<br>FVRCP booster |
| 16 weeks: | Rabies virus, if required, then yearly<br>FVRCP booster<br>Infectious Peritonitis (FIP), only for high risk environments. |

Note: It takes one to two weeks for immunity to develop. I will need booster shots every one to three years. Other inoculations and heartworm preventative may be recommended by my veterinarian based on our location and my breed.

As an adult cat I should see my veterinarian once a year or when I have a problem. You and my veterinarian are now **partners** in promoting my good health! The following are a few suggestions for successful visits to my veterinarian.

- Tell the receptionist the nature of our visit when making an appointment.
- Make a list of questions for the veterinarian before our visit, and be prepared to answer questions about my health.
- Ask for written instructions about my care and medications. If you do not understand the instructions, ask for clarification before we leave.

# PAWS to consider

**MY NEW HOME.** Adjusting to a new environment is stressful for me. The Christmas holidays are an especially difficult time to introduce me to my new home, since this is a hectic time for everyone. If I am intended to be a holiday gift, it is best to bring me home the day after Christmas. My first impressions of my new home are important, and I will need your full attention for the first few days.

Before bringing me home, take time to prepare children for my arrival and kitty-proof my new home. (See PAWS to consider/CHILDREN, page 26, and PAWS to consider/SAFETY, page 32.) When picking me up from the breeder, take my carrier and an old towel with you. Ask the breeder to gently rub the towel against my mother's fur to absorb her scent. Place the towel in the bottom of my carrier and then in my bed at home. I will be comforted by the scent. Obtain my medical records from the breeder as well as my feeding schedule, kind of food and type of litter I am using. Once I am home, train me to be an indoor cat. (See PAWS to consider/TRAINING, page 62.) Allow me outdoors only with supervision, and never permit me outdoors in inclement weather or when temperatures are extremely hot or cold.

During **the first week**, the following suggestions are helpful for my successful adjustment:

- Establish a routine. We kittens are creatures of habit and will grow into more secure and confident cats when we can rely on a regular daily routine.
- Give me time to rest in private and restrict visitors.
- Keep me from socializing with other household pets because they might contract an illness from me or vice versa. Confine me to a separate area with my toys, feeding bowls, litter box, scratching post, and bed. After my immunizations have taken effect, gradually introduce me to the other pets with your constant supervision. If a dog is in the household, restrain it with a leash until we become accustomed to each other. When in the presence of a dog, always provide a safe place for me to retreat. Do not let the dog bark and scare me. Give the other pets plenty of attention so they will not be jealous.
- Keep a watchful eye on my eating and drinking habits. If there are other cats in the household, I should have my own feeding bowl and litter box.
- Feed me the same food I have been eating. If you decide to change my food or litter, do so gradually. (See PAWS to consider/FEEDING, page 38 and LITTER BOX TRAINING, page 44.)
- Supervise small children's time with me. Do not permit them to carry me because they may drop me. (See PAWS to consider/CHILDREN, page 26.)
- Take me for a veterinary exam. Bring my medical records and a fecal sample to test for parasites. (See PAWS to consider/MY VETERINARIAN, page 19.)
- Check state and local laws concerning cat ownership.

Note: Travel is very stressful for cats. It is not wise for me to travel until I am at least three months old. (See PAWS to consider/TRAVEL, page 90.)

## PURRsonals

Before coming to my new home, I was examined by my breeder's
veterinarian who left the following advice for my new "parent(s)":

_____

_____

To make me feel at home, my "parent(s)" bought the following for me:

_____

_____

Shortly after acquiring me, my "parent(s)" took me to my new veterinarian.
(See PAWS to consider/MY VETERINARIAN, page 19, for complete list of immunizations
and MY HEALTH CARE RECORD, page 116.)

My veterinarian gave my "parent(s)" the following advice:_____

_____

During my exam, I purred, yowled, shook, lost hair, hissed, clawed, tried to bite the vet, was

"cool" (circle all that apply) or I _____

I was checked for worms and was found to have _____

I must take the following medications:_____

_____

for_____        _____

at the following times: _____

When the visit was over, my vet gave me _____

My "parent(s)" gave me a big hug, a treat, my favorite toy, or a "good kitty" pat (circle

one or more) or_____

## PAWS to consider

SUPPLIES. Supplies I will need:

- **A bed.** My bed can be as plain or fancy as you choose. A cardboard box containing a washable rug, blanket, or pillow for warmth is sufficient. Cut a section from the side of the box for my easy access. On the fancy side, a cat owner can find beanbag and hammock cat beds as well as cozy, covered beds lined with fleece. Whatever type of bed you choose, make sure there are no protruding objects that could injure me. (See PAWS to consider/SLEEPING, page 42.)

- **A sturdy scratching post** made of soft plain wood, cardboard or wood covered with sisal rope or short nap carpeting. Karate Kat™ (800-822-6628) produces top quality posts. A post is needed for exercise and to renew my front claws. It should be tall enough to accommodate my full height as an adult cat, when I stand on my hind legs. A cat treat can be placed on top of the scratching post to entice me to use it.

- **A roomy and well-ventilated cat carrier** for taking me to the veterinarian or when we travel. The carrier should be large enough to accommodate me when I am full grown. I should be able to stand up and turn around in the carrier. Make sure there are no sharp protrusions or areas where I can snag my collar. The authors prefer plastic carriers. (See PAWS to consider/TRAVEL, page 90.)

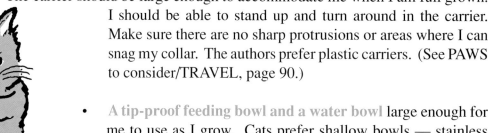

- **A tip-proof feeding bowl and a water bowl** large enough for me to use as I grow. Cats prefer shallow bowls — stainless steel bowls are best. Ceramic bowls are cute and all right to use if manufactured in the United States. Otherwise, the glaze may contain lead, which is toxic. Plastic bowls can wear and harbor bacteria in the cracks. In addition, some cats develop allergies to the plastic.

- **A large litter box, litter, and a scoop or tongs for removing fecal matter.** Use a rectangular plastic box that has plenty of digging room and enough length to accommodate me when I am an adult cat. If I am too small to climb into the box, use an aluminum or plastic pan with a two-inch rim until I am older. The litter box can be covered or uncovered. A covered box is best if there is a dog in the house with a fondness for cat feces. Self-cleaning litter boxes are available, but they are costly. Use litter made from unscented clay or sand with small granules. Most cats do not like scented litter and some develop allergies to the scent. **Litter box liners** are very convenient but not a necessity. My claws can rip holes in the liner. **Baking soda** can be sprinkled under the litter to absorb odors. Do not use Lysol which contains ethanol or any disinfectant with phenol. These are toxic to cats. (See PAWS to consider/LITTER BOX TRAINING, page 44.)

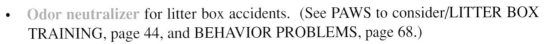

- Odor neutralizer for litter box accidents. (See PAWS to consider/LITTER BOX TRAINING, page 44, and BEHAVIOR PROBLEMS, page 68.)

- Grooming tools. A short-haired cat needs a natural, short-bristle brush, a slicker brush and a rubber curry brush. A long-haired cat needs a slicker brush, a stainless steel wide-toothed comb with blunt tips and a natural, long-bristle brush. Coat conditioner spray controls static electricity during grooming. (See PAWS to consider/GROOMING, page 47.)

- A claw clipper, and styptic pencil (for claw clipping accidents). (See PAWS to consider/PETicures, page 50.)

- Blunt-nosed scissors or hair trimming equipment, if my breed requires these.

- Products for cleaning my teeth include either sterile pads and oral cleansing solution, or a feline toothbrush and toothpaste. (See PAWS to consider/DENTAL HYGIENE, page 51.)

- Tartar control treats or treats specifically for cats. Human food treats are not necessary and will make me fat. All treats should be given in moderation. If the moisture content exceeds 12%, the treats may cause diarrhea for some of us. (See PAWS to consider/FEEDING, page 38.)

- Toys that are safe for chewing and playtime. Soft cloth catnip toys, ping-pong balls, cardboard boxes with openings to allow me to explore; paper bags for hiding; or old knotted socks are some good examples of safe toys. Toys should be large enough that they cannot become lodged in my throat or swallowed. Toys should not have squeakers, bells, or small parts that I can remove and should be appropriate to my size. (See PAWS to consider/SAFETY, page 32 and PAWS to consider/PLAY/EXERCISE, page 79.)

- Small squirt gun or compressed air gun for training. Do not use a power squirt gun because the force of the water could hurt me.

- Products to prevent me from chewing on plants or cords, such as Grannick's Bitter Apple® or Four Paws® Cat Repellent.

- A first aid kit and first aid book for cats. (See SOME PURRfectly GOOD ADVICE, page 110.)

- Bathing products. Use <u>feline</u> flea and tick shampoo, if needed. At all other times, use a mild <u>feline</u> shampoo. Keep clean towels handy for my use only. Use sterile pads and ear cleaning solution for ear care. Bathing products will seldom be needed, so buy small quantities. (See PAWS to consider/BATHING, page 54.)

24

- **A collar with identification (I.D.), a figure 8 or an H-shaped cat harness and a lightweight leather or cord leash.** My collar should have an elasticized section that will allow me to free myself if I become entangled with an object. To assure proper  collar fit: measure the circumference of my neck and add two inches. Continue to adjust the size of my collar as I grow. A rolled collar is best if I am long-haired. I should always wear my collar with attached I.D. tag listing my name, my address and phone number. My I.D. tag will prevent me from being mistaken for a stray if I should escape and become lost. If I refuse to wear a collar, use a harness designed for cats. Attach an I.D. tag to the harness. Use the harness and leash for training and transporting me. To assure proper harness fit: measure the circumference of my body immediately behind my forelegs and add two inches. Using a leash that is no longer than four feet allows you to keep me under control. If I refuse to wear a collar or harness, I need another form of identification. (See PAWS to consider/LOST KITTIES, page 96.) (Miss Flori can disengage herself from a collar in less than five seconds and fling it far enough to easily score a field goal. When it comes to a harness, forget it. She only tolerates it for veterinary visits.)

- **Prescribed medications,** if needed.

**Supplies that would be nice to have:**

- **Outdoor enclosure.** If you want me to spend time outdoors, keep me safe by providing a secure exercise enclosure with a sturdy roof and shelter that protects me from inclement weather. The enclosure should be placed in a shady area; have several wide perches at varying heights; toys, a litter box, and food and water bowls. Place a washable rug in the shelter for warmth and comfort. Cover the enclosure with wire mesh that cannot be spread apart. The wire mesh should be small enough to prevent me from getting my paw caught and to keep other animals from reaching me. I should not be placed in my outdoor enclosure during severe weather. (See PAWS to consider/ Some PURRfectly Good Advice, page 111, concerning cat enclosure kits.)

- **Electric indoor fencing** is very affordable and successful for confining me to an area of the house where I cannot claw fine furnishings.

- **A spoon and fork** to be used for my food only. **A rubber mat** under both food and water bowls to prevent messes.

- **A book** on my specific breed.

- **A window perch or cat tree** with several ledges for lounging or for viewing the outdoor world.

MY FIRST PHOTO IN MY NEW HOME

MY REGISTRATION CERTIFICATE
OR ANOTHER PHOTO

26

**PAWS to consider**

**CHILDREN AND KITTIES.** Most children are attracted to kittens like a magnet. However, I will not be fond of toddlers who do not have total control of their movements and can inadvertently hurt me. A toddler's shrill scream can frighten me, and I may try to defend myself by scratching and biting. Introduce me gradually to an infant or toddler, and <u>always</u> monitor our time together. By teaching the children how to relate to me in a positive, responsible, and calm manner, you make it possible for me to interact with all members of the family, regardless of their ages.

Children should be taught that I am not a toy, but an addition to the family who must be treated gently and kindly. Show a child how to pick me up by placing one hand under my chest, behind my forelegs, and one hand under my hind quarters for support. Have the child lift me into the crook of an arm. **No one** should pick me up by the scruff of my neck, by my tail, or one leg.

Give all children in the household, depending on their ages and capabilities, the responsibility of taking care of one of my needs, such as feeding or exercise. The children must learn a few simple rules to protect other small household pets from me. Making sure that lids on small pets' cages are secure should be one of the children's responsibilities. Litter box duties should be left to the older children. Parasites, such as roundworm, can be transmitted from my fecal material to humans so, teach children to wash their hands after cleaning my litter box. (See PAWS to consider/PARASITES, page 59.) By caring for me, children learn about responsible pet ownership, experience compassion and have a sense of accomplishment. Let the children accompany us when we visit the veterinarian so they can comfort me and be part of my total care.

For the first month or two, I will tire easily. When I become tired, allow me to rest quietly. Children should be taught not to bother me when I am sleeping. If I am awakened suddenly, I may be disoriented and protect myself by scratching. Likewise, I should be left alone when I am eating or using the litter box. Teach the children how to play with me gently. No squeezing, chasing, pinching, poking, pulling my tail or limbs; falling on top of me; or shouting at me. Explain to the children that they would not like to be mistreated or bitten when I defend myself. Cats do not enjoy roughhousing. Therefore, the best way to play with me is by sitting on the floor and interacting with me at my level.

Because I am an independent creature, I march to a drumbeat that is uniquely my own. I may enjoy having the children cuddle me for a short while; then, I must be free to roam the house, explore, and play. I should be put down gently when I begin to struggle to be free. If treated kindly and responsibly, I will be a child's devoted friend; a comfort during sad times; and an added joy during good times.

**TABBY TIPS**

My Tail Tells Tales
Tail Waving Slowly =
Happy Cat
Tail Held High =
Greeting Cat
Tail Swishing =
Annoyed Cat
Tail Held Low =
Angry Cat
Tail Arched & Fluffed =
Scared Cat

I greet you in my special way,
With twitching tail and eyes so bright.
My kitty joy is unrestrained;
I'm loudly purring with delight!

Your gentle voice, your friendly touch,
Are kindly gestures I adore.
I'm happy when our play begins,
And you're with me once more.

I don't care if we're in the chips,
Or out of luck and destitute;
My wealth is knowing I'm all yours,
And that our friendship's absolute!

**BECAUSE I'M YOUR KITTY!**

# MY PAW PRINTS

To make prints, use food coloring or other non-toxic material.  Make prints on separate pieces of paper.  Affix to this page using a glue stick.  Be sure to rinse my feet afterwards.

FORE LEFT

FORE RIGHT

HIND LEFT

HIND RIGHT

SNIP OF MY HAIR

PHOTOS OF ME WITH MY NEW FAMILY

## TWO TO THREE MONTHS

I weigh _____.  I am _____tall.
(measure from floor to top of shoulder)

My "parent(s)" bought these supplies for me:_____

_____

_____

To pamPURR me, my "parent(s)" bought: _____

_____

This month I've learned: _____

_____

I first wore my collar at _____ months.

I recognized my name at _____ months.

I recognized my family at _____ months.

I purr when _____

I meow when _____

I growl when _____

Other pet members in my family include _____

Their names are _____

_____

The other pets think I am _____

I think the other pets are_____

I interact with the resident dog(s) or other cat(s) by grooming them _____ playing

with them _____ sharing a bed _____.

# PHOTOS OF ME DOING ADORABLE KITTY STUFF

**P**AWS to consider

SAFETY. We kitties are very curious. Please do not let that curiosity kill me. Make it difficult for me to be injured or get into trouble. Protect me and your belongings by looking at the house and yard from my level and removing any potentially dangerous objects. The following are some suggestions for kitten-proofing our home:

- **Remove small area rugs and bath mats that I can hide beneath.** You might not see me and could accidentally step on me. In fact, since I am so small, walk carefully. I love to get underfoot and could cause you to trip. We both could be seriously injured. When you walk, do the slow kitty shuffle!

- **Block unused electrical outlets with guard plugs.** Tape electrical wires and cords (including phone cords) to the floor or baseboard. Spray the wires or cords with an anti-chew product, such as Grannick's Bitter Apple® or Four Paws® Cat Repellent. If cords are attached to heavy objects, secure the objects so I cannot pull the cord and cause the object to fall on top of me.

- **Secure loose drapery cords** so I cannot become entangled and possibly hang myself. Toss the drapes and shower curtains over the rod for a few months to discourage me from climbing them.

- **Keep screenless windows closed.** I could escape, become lost, or fall from the windowsill. Cats do not always land on their feet and, if the fall is high enough, I could be seriously injured or killed. For the same reason, never allow me onto a balcony. If windows have screens, make sure they are secure. We cats excel at creating openings.

**TABBY TIPS**

Unfortunately, about 14% of all cats' deaths are the result of falls!

- **Remove all toxic substances from my area** including soaps and cosmetics. Secure cupboards with child-proof locks, if needed. When cleaning areas where I walk, be sure to rinse thoroughly. I can absorb the cleaning substance through my paws and ingest it while grooming myself. Remove all moth balls. We cats are attracted to moth balls because they are fun to play with and taste good to us. Never allow me to drink alcohol products.

- **Remove yarn, string, sewing thread, dental floss and continuous filament carpeting from my area.** These items can strand out and cause an intestinal blockage. If you see one of these items extending from either end of my anatomy, do not pull it! You could cause severe internal damage. Take me to my veterinarian <u>immediately</u>. This is an emergency!

- **Remove valuable and breakable objects from my area.** I can injure a paw if I walk on broken objects. Healing a cut on a paw is difficult and can take weeks. Some objects can be secured with double-sided tape or Pet Proof Putty™. The putty is safe for use on any finished surface. (For a store that sells the putty, call 800-959-4053.)

- **Remove dangerous items that I could chew and swallow,** for example, thumbtacks, needles, buttons, paper clips, cellophane, aluminum foil, pins, aluminum can tabs, rubber bands, baby bottle nipples, and pacifiers. As a kitten I will chew anything I can get my jaws around; particularly, when I am teething between three and six months of age. Think like a **kitten!** Look for items that might attract me. Of special concern are cigarette butts, sharp or glass objects, chocolate, <u>all medications; especially aspirin or drugs containing acetaminophen, such as Tylenol®</u>. Chocolate contains theobromine, a substance that is toxic to cats. Replace my toys as soon as they start to fall apart. Confine me to a kitty-safe room when I cannot be supervised.

- **Check boxes or luggage before storing.** I may be hiding inside.

- **Keep closets, cabinets, and drawers closed.** I can climb into a drawer and be injured if the drawer is slammed shut. If necessary, install child-proof latches to cabinet doors. Always look for me before closing any door.

- **Do not leave the door to the clothes dryer, trash compactor, washing machine, dishwasher, or oven open.** As a precaution, check thoroughly for me before starting any appliance or machine where I may be hiding. Look for me in the refrigerator or freezer before closing the door.

- **Check a sofa bed or a recliner chair before folding it** to make sure I am not inside the bed or under the chair. I can be crushed in the mechanical operation. Watch out for my paws and tail when using a rocking chair.

- **Block stairways**, especially those going down; and all small spaces where I can hide or hurt myself. Place double-sided tape directly in front of the space.

- **Do not let me socialize with other pets until my inoculations take effect.** It takes one to two weeks after a vaccine is given to activate immunity.

- **Remove all plastic bags from my area.** I could suffocate if I crawl into one, or choke on pieces I have torn from a bag.

- **Remove all plants from my reach.** We kitties like to snack on houseplants. When I am older, you can return the non-poisonous plants to my areas. Grannick's Bitter Apple®, a bio-degradable product, can be safely sprayed on plants and keeps me from chewing them. (See SOME PURRfectly GOOD ADVICE, page 114, for information about poisonous plants.) If you allow me outdoors for supervised play, guard me against poisonous plants and substances, such as slug or rat poison. Ask lawn service personnel how soon I can safely be outdoors after they have treated the grass or bushes. Be aware of the safety instructions on all garden products you use.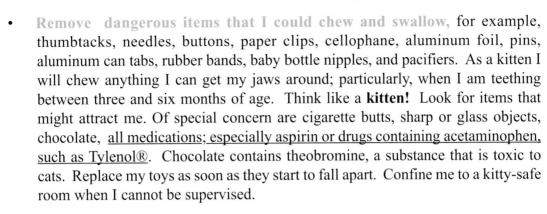

- **After you finish eating, store all food items and used utensils.** Remove all open cans and lids, sharp knives or food processor blades; especially if there is food on them. I will be attracted to the food which could result in a severe cut on my tongue or mouth. If you use steel wool to clean pans, store it in a safe area. The smell of food may remain on the steel wool and I may eat it.

- **Put all toilet covers down.** I may be tempted to drink from the toilets. Toilet bowl cleaners, including the type that hang in the tank, are toxic. After cleaning the toilet, flush it a few times to remove any cleaning residue. A small kitten can drown if it falls into a toilet, a tub or basin filled with water.

- **Securely cover all garbage cans** or remove them from my reach.

- **Stabilize all objects and furniture.** Jumping on furniture or from one object to another is great fun for me unless the object I am jumping to is unsteady. The piece of furniture could fall on me and cause injury. (Note: Cats can leap five times their body length from the standing position.)

- **Do not line my bed with an electric blanket.** I might chew on the wires and electrocute myself. There are heating devices designed for cats.

- **Do not light fires or candles where I can reach them.** Cover all fireplaces with screens. This will also keep me from climbing up the inside of the chimney or playing in the ashes. Protect me from a hot iron, barbecue grill, hot oven door and stove tops. Covers are available for stove tops.

- **Put "Animal on Premises" stickers on the front and back doors of our house.** In case of fire, the sticker will alert firefighters to my presence. If we move to another home, be sure to remove the stickers from the doors of the old house. We would not want firefighters spending time searching for me when I am no longer there. Have a rescue plan for all pets in the household in case of natural disaster or fire. (See PAWS to consider/Some PURRfectly good advice, page 111.)

- **Always use break-away collars** so there is no possibility that I could hang myself. An H-shaped cat harness is more secure and safe. Never leave a leash on me when I am unattended. Attach my identification tag to my collar or my harness. Do not place a ribbon around my neck, no matter how adorable I look, because it could snag on an object and hang me.

- **Keep Christmas trees, packages, tinsel, ornaments, and ornament hooks out of my reach.** If you cannot keep me out of the room that contains the Christmas tree, place plastic carpet runners, bumpy side up, around the tree. Cats do not like the feel of hard plastic on their paws. Keep potential launching pads, such as tables, away from the tree. Do not tempt me by decorating the tree with edible items, such as popcorn. Cover the water at the base of the tree because it can be toxic.

- **Introduce me to the resident canine after I adjust to my new home.** For the first week or two, keep me in an area away from the dog and give it extra attention to prevent jealousy. When the dog is outdoors, give me more freedom. Take something of mine and place it in the dog's bed and vice versa to acquaint us with each other's scent. When the time is right to introduce us, trim my front claws. If I scratch the dog, it will not have kind thoughts about me the next time we meet. When introducing us, restrain the dog and provide me with a safe retreat. It is natural for a dog to want to chase a cat. Regardless of the dog's size or age, do not give it the opportunity to chase me or you will spoil our budding relationship. Some breeds are bred to kill vermin and may consider me prey. Likewise, it is important to keep me from stalking the dog. After we are accustomed to each other, we still require supervision because a dog can accidentally injure a tiny kitten. When I am full grown and familiar with the house, I can usually hold my own. If a problem continues, it is wise to seek professional training for the dog. Dogs and cats usually coexist peacefully if introduced properly. (Miss Flori lives with two dogs and Dale lives with one.)

- **Train me to stay indoors.** (See PAWS to Consider/TRAINING, page 62.) If I am an outdoor cat, the length of my life is directly proportionate to the number of automobiles, dogs, tom cats, coyotes, hawks, toxic substances, and parasites in my neighborhood. It is not cruel to keep me indoors. In fact, it shows the highest regard for me. An indoor cat is secure and happy having a few window perches with a view of the outside world. In a cold climate, an outdoor cat may seek warmth from a car engine only to be severely injured when the engine is started. The sweet taste of antifreeze, which is extremely toxic, will attract a cat. An outdoor cat can fall into an uncovered swimming pool and drown, be injured by broken glass and other dangerous objects in the yard or poisoned by substances in the yard or garden. A cat may use the children's sandbox as a litter box, thus jeopardizing the children's health if the cat has parasites. Black cats are sometimes victims of cruel acts at Halloween. Firecrackers associated with the Fourth of July are very frightening and may cause a cat to run off and be lost.

# PURRsonals

My "parent(s)" cat-proofed our house by _____

_____

My nosiness gets me into trouble when _____

_____

I knocked over _____

I climbed into _____

I tried to eat _____

I fell into _____

When my "parent(s)" sees me getting into trouble, I hide in _____,

behind _____, under the _____ or

_____

I responded to the word "No!" at _____ months, when I was about to

_____

When I responded, my "parent(s)" gave me _____

I like to explore _____

I like to hide behind _____

I like to get under _____

I like to climb _____

I like to jump over _____

or crawl under _____

I like to chew _____

I got stuck behind _____

and my "parent(s)" had to _____

When I am all tuckered out from my adventures, my favorite place to take a cat nap is

_____

# PHOTOS OF ME DINING

PAWS to consider

**FEEDING.** Unlike humans, I have only one year to mature into an adult. It is, therefore, important to choose a <u>high-quality, nutritionally complete kitten</u> food for me during my first year and a nutritionally balanced cat food thereafter. During the first week, feed me the same food that was fed to me by my breeder and on the same schedule. Otherwise, I may have an upset tummy. After a week, if you wish to change my type of kitten food, introduce the new food slowly, mixing it with the food you are already giving me. Observe my bowel movements. If the stool is loose or I am straining, my diet is being changed too rapidly. Changing my food too often can make me a finicky eater.

### TABBY TIPS
Use foods tested by the Association of American Feed Control Officials (look for endorsement on package.)

Cats are carnivorous; therefore, my diet must be meat-based. There are three types of food available for kittens: canned, semi-moist, and dry. If you choose a canned kitten food, always cover and refrigerate the unused portion so it will not spoil. Because most cats do not like cold food, let the unused portion warm to room temperature or heat it in a microwave-safe container before feeding. If you choose a semi-moist food, consult my veterinarian to make sure it does not contain an excess of sugar and chemicals. Dry kitten food is nutritionally balanced; easy to store; better for my teeth; and the most economical when bought in large quantities. Whichever type of food you choose, it should contain taurine, an amino acid required for normal feline vision and a healthy heart. With nutritionally balanced food, I do not need vitamin supplements. Never give me food that contains bones. Bones can splinter, causing gastrointestinal problems. Do not feed me raw meat because it may harbor harmful parasites. I should not be fed dog food because it does not have enough protein for cats. Dogs in our household should not be allowed to eat my food or bother me while I am eating. Place my food bowls out of their reach. Consult my veterinarian about the amount and type of food that is best for me.

Follow the feeding guidelines on the kitten food package — but be flexible! Very active kittens may need more food. When there is more than one cat in our household, each of us should have its own food and water bowls and be fed in separate areas. Always feed me from the same bowl, in the same location, and at the same time each day. Thoroughly clean my bowl before putting food in it. Place the food bowl in a quiet, low traffic area away from my litter box. Leave my food bowl down for thirty minutes. After thirty minutes, remove the bowl even if I have not eaten. Take me to my litter box and leave me alone. Using the box shortly after a meal helps me develop good eating and toilet habits. Allow time for my food to digest before engaging me in play. Until I am three months of age, feed me four times per day. From three to six months of age, feed me three times per day. At six months and beyond, feed me twice per day or consider self-feeding, which makes my daily allowance of food available at all times. The self-feeding method can only be used with foods that do not require refrigeration. (See PAWS to consider/ ONE YEAR AND BEYOND, page 102.) Self-feeding may not work, if there is more than one cat in our home and may even create competition for the food. If you feed me in an outdoor enclosure, bowls are available that keep ants out of my food and water. A moat is concealed under the bowl. Water and a few drops of liquid soap are added to the moat to prevent ants from crossing it.

Give treats as a reward during training or for good behavior. However, giving me too many treats can spoil my appetite and prevent me from eating the nutritional foods I need for growth. A few tartar-control treats can be given each day to promote healthier teeth and gums. (See PAWS to consider/DENTAL HYGIENE, page 51.) Tartar control treats are especially important if I am eating soft food. Give tuna or other seafood treats very sparingly because they contain a high level of magnesium which can contribute to the formation of crystals in the urine. These crystals can block the urinary tract.

I may meow pleadingly for your left-overs, but don't ever fall for that ploy. Feeding me my food at the same time you eat reduces my tendency to beg. Train me to stay off the dining table or you may find me drinking from your glass or trying to snatch food from your plate. (See PAWS to consider/TRAINING, page 62.) "People food" is not nutritionally balanced for me and some foods, such as onions or chocolate, can be toxic — or even fatal. Feeding me "people food" will not make me love you more. It will make me fat and ruin my teeth. I will become a candidate for weight-related problems like heart disease, urinary blockage and diabetes. A fatty diet is also a cause of flatulence. You should not let me gain more than 10% over my ideal weight. My ribs should not show, yet you should be able to feel them without pressing too hard. Gaining too much weight is easy, but taking it off is not. Sound familiar? If I have a weight problem, even though I am being fed correctly and exercised regularly, consult my veterinarian. She may suggest a cat food lower in fat. Always consult my veterinarian concerning dramatic weight loss or gain. I may have a medical problem.

Even though I am a well-fed cat, do not make the mistake of thinking that I will not prey upon smaller animals. Hunting is instinctive for all cats and I will hunt no matter how well-fed I am, or how balanced a diet I receive. Make sure that I do not gain access to areas where other household pets such as gerbils, hamsters, or birds live. Keep lids tightly closed on small animal cages. My authors believe that, because domestic cats are not a natural part of the environment, they should be seen on the street only when walking on a leash with their owners. This insures that I remain under control and do not wantonly kill or maim lovely song birds or other small wildlife that may have diseases which can be transmitted to me. In turn, I can pass some of these diseases on to you.

Cool, fresh water should be available to me at all times and in more than one location. I will need more water if I am fed dry food. Sufficient amounts of water help prevent urinary tract problems. Male cats are especially prone to such problems. Make sure my water bowls are always clean. Do not substitute milk for water. In fact, I do not need milk. I may have a problem digesting it and develop diarrhea.

# FAT CAT

She's coming from the grocery store;
I'll rest here on the kitchen floor.
She knows that I'm a carnivore
**IN THE KITCHEN**.

I'll just pretend to be asleep;
My sense of smell will help me keep
In touch with rhythm, pulse and beat
**IN THE KITCHEN**.

Aromas have such great appeal;
I hope that tuna's my next meal.
And I will borrow, beg, or steal
**IN THE KITCHEN**.

I have no more fulfilling wish,
Than to discover in my dish,
A chicken or filet of fish
**IN THE KITCHEN**.

I'll lift one eye and take a peek;
It could be chickie that I seek!
She looks my way; she's going to speak
**IN THE KITCHEN**.

"Hey, Fat Cat, you are really sly;
There's not a trick that you won't try
To get your paws on fish I fry
**IN THE KITCHEN**."

Your kitten food will keep you fit,
Each bite and morsel, every bit.
Good food and kisses we permit
**IN THE KITCHEN**.

# PURRsonals

I eat _____ times a day, in the _____, with _____

I eat _____ chow.

My favorite treat is _____

I get a treat when _____

_____

My favorite "people food" is _____ (In spite of my "parent's" best efforts to keep me on a feline diet, I discovered "people food.")

I got into a box of _____, a can of _____,

a bag of _____, a dish of _____

This is what happened: _____

_____

_____

My "parent(s)" said, "_____

_____. "

In spite of my "discoveries," my "parent(s)" still thinks I am _____

_____

I sleep in a _____, on a _____, under a

_____, by my _____, with my _____

The first time I slept through the night was _____

When I sleep

| | |
|---|---|
| my paw jerks | _____ |
| my ears tremble | _____ |
| I growl | _____ |
| I purr | _____ |
| my tail twitches | _____ |

# PAWS to consider

**SLEEPING.** Cats have never been known to suffer from insomnia. In fact, cats have elevated naps to an art form. Frequent and regular <u>uninterrupted</u> sleep is very necessary to my health.

When I am tired, where can I rest my weary head? I would appreciate a warm, comfortable, clean bed intended just for me. Drafts and dampness are not good for my health. While I am a kitten, a cardboard box will suffice. Make sure that the sides are high enough to give me a sense of security. Put a rug under the box if the floor is drafty. Cut an opening in one side of the box for my doorway. Place a washable rug or pillow in the box. I am used to snuggling with my mom and littermates, so I need something warm and cozy as a substitute. If you purchase a bed, make sure it is large enough to accommodate me as a full grown cat. I should be able to stretch out while lying down. The bed should be washable and have sides that prevent drafts. Visit our local pet store and ask if you can return a bed if I do not like it. It may take several tries before you get one I like. (See PAWS to consider/SUPPLIES, page 22).

Place my bed in a quiet area away from traffic. Whenever you find me sleeping somewhere that is unacceptable, take me to my bed. As a kitten, I enjoy climbing in and out of things; therefore, I may seek out hidden places for a nap. There may be times when you cannot find me, but if you have kitty-proofed my areas, I will eventually emerge safe and sound (see PAWS to consider/ SAFETY, page 32). On average, a cat sleeps sixteen hours per day.

At night, you can place my bed near your bed; however, I will probably prefer sleeping with you. If this is not your cup of tea, place me back in my bed. Brush or stroke me for a few minutes before returning to your bed — repeat as needed. If I refuse to stay in my bed, move my bed to another room of the house and then close the door to that room. Be prepared for some loud meowing. The next night place my bed in your room again and go through the same procedure. Eventually, I will figure out what you want, or you will give up and let me sleep with you.

## MY KITTY CAT NAP ATTACK

We cats can nap behind a door,
Beneath your bed, or on the floor.

If we are young, and not too fat,
We like to sleep in baseball hats.

Some can vanish like a vapor.
Others lie on your newspaper.

Some like to sleep upon a lap,
While others like a sunny nap.

A kitty found inside a bowl
Can surely try a person's soul!

A Nap Attack, therefore, can be,
In any place that pleases me!

# PHOTOS OF ME TAKING A SNOOZE

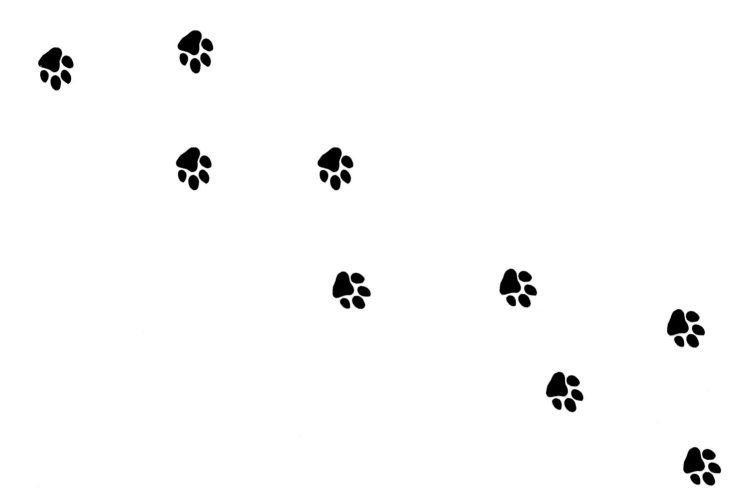

# PAWS to consider

**LITTER BOX TRAINING.** Before coming to my new home, my mother probably taught me how to use a litter box. If not, start the litter box training as soon as I come home with you. Teach me by taking me to my litter box about every two hours and gently moving my front paws through the litter so I understand the idea of digging. Take me to my litter box as soon as I finish eating. Always make my litter box accessible. Praise me by petting and talking to me every time I use it. Do not let me have the run of the house until I have established good litter box habits. (See PAWS to consider/SUPPLIES, page 22, for more information on litter, litter box liners, disinfectants, and litter boxes).

Small cats need about one inch of litter in the bottom of the litter box. Large cats need two inches of litter. Remove feces daily. When using the clumping type litter, remove the wet clumps and replace with fresh litter. Once a week the litter should be changed and the litter box washed with mild unscented soap and hot water. When cleaning a litter box, it is

possible to contract toxoplasmosis — a disease carried by cats. If contracted by a pregnant woman, it can cause birth defects. Usually, indoor cats do not have this parasite because it is contracted when cats eat birds, rodents, or raw meat. You can have me tested for toxoplasmosis. If I do have this disease, consult your doctor about the possibility of wearing plastic gloves while cleaning the box. It takes one to five days for toxoplasmosis to become infectious in feces, so cleaning the litter daily may reduce the chance of becoming infected. Whether I have a disease or not, everyone should wash his or her hands thoroughly after cleaning a litter box.

Until I have established good litter box habits, keep large houseplants out of my reach. I may be tempted to use them as my toilet! You can cover the soil area with double-sided tape or wire mesh. Always cover the front of a fireplace. Ashes are very tempting "litter boxes" for kittens. Block off areas leading to the back of large pieces of furniture or other out-of-the-way private places that I might choose as a toilet. Provide a litter box for each cat in our household. A multi-level house should have a litter box on each level. Locate my litter box in a quiet, private area separate from my feeding bowls. A bathroom is a good location; especially, when flushable litter is used. The laundry room may not be a good choice if I am frightened by the sound of the washer or dryer. If the family dog likes cat feces, place the litter box in a closet. Install a cat door into the closet door, or use a door stopper to adjust the closet door, so only I can enter. A covered litter box may provide another solution. When I am outdoors for supervised play, I should not be allowed to use the children's sandbox or the garden as a litter box.

Occasionally, I will forget where the litter box is and have an accident. If you catch me in the act of going potty outside the litter box, clap your hands loudly and say, "NO!" firmly. Pick me up and take me to my litter box. Place me inside the box. When I use the box, praise me lavishly and give me a treat. I may not use it at this time, but a treat will reinforce the idea of using it in the future.

Clean the accident area and disinfect it with an odor neutralizer. You must use a neutralizer. Even if you cannot detect an odor, I can. My sense of smell is much stronger than yours. If the area is not properly neutralized, I may be attracted to it again. If you discover an accident after the fact, simply clean it up and disinfect the area. Scolding will do no good because I am not able to associate my misdeed with the punishment. If I continue to have problems, change the type of litter you are using and clean my box more often. Cats do not like a dirty litter box. Consult my veterinarian about the problem. I may have a medical disorder that requires attention. A low-grade urinary tract infection, an upset tummy, or worms can cause me to have elimination problems. Sometimes stress or loneliness can cause me to have accidents. Plan on spending more time with me each day. There is <u>NO</u> valid argument for the use of hands to shake, swat, spank, or wield a rolled up newspaper in litter box training or <u>ANY</u> other aspect of your relationship with me. Keep in mind that I am still a baby. **(The authors feel that rubbing a kitty's nose in its mistake is cruel. They believe that it does nothing except humiliate the kitty and lessen the bond between the kitty and its owner.)**

(Miss Flori was approximately ten months old when she was rescued by Jodi. Miss Flori had very definite ideas about what she liked. When Jodi tried a covered litter box with recycled paper, Miss Flori made some very convincing arguments on the floor next to the litter box. She now happily uses an open box with unscented clay litter. When Kathy rescued Dale, he was a sickly stray that had collapsed on her patio. While Dale was making the transition from outdoor to indoor cat, he refused to use a litter box until Kathy added two cups of yard soil to the unscented clumping type of litter in his box. Over a two-to-three week period, the soil was continually decreased until he accepted the litter.)

If you have a great deal of patience, it is possible to train me to use the toilet. Check the local pet store for information and the required equipment.

## DON'T DO IT THERE

I potty on the rug and someone points to my mistake;
A loud and angry voice can make a little kitty quake!

I cannot think in human terms or know the value of
The rugs and carpets in the room, possessions that you love.

I have a language of my own, as all my actions show;
My body language says it all, a "cat speak" you should know.

So when I must relieve myself, remember things are new;
Be sure to have my litter box directly in my view.

Just use a scoop and plastic bag; clean up my residue.
Although cats are fastidious, we still depend on YOU!

THREE TO FOUR MONTHS

I weigh _____. I am _____ tall.

This month I've learned: _____

_____

I visited my veterinarian on _____
(I need additional inoculations at this time)

I learned to negotiate stairs at _____ months.

My method for going down the stairs was _____

I follow _____ up or down the stairs.

My "parent(s)" does not mind if I jump to the top of _____

My "parent(s)" does not like it when I leap to _____

_____

To discourage me, my "parent(s)" _____

_____

I give myself a bath every_____

My "parent(s)" grooms me every _____

When groomed, the part I like best is _____

I do not like baths, but I needed one because _____

When I was bathed, I yowled _____; hissed _____; growled _____;

sat dejectedly _____;  embedded my claws in the drywall and headed for the ceiling

_____; or _____

When my "parent(s)" trimmed my claws, I was most cooperative_____; wiggled constantly

_____; cried _____; acted like the world was coming to an end _____;

or _____
(See PAWS to consider/PETicures, page 50.)

My "parent(s)" brushed my teeth the first time when I was _____ months old.

I cooperated/I did not cooperate (circle one).

# PAWS to consider

**GROOMING.** Grooming creates a special bond between us and is essential for my health. Grooming should consist of the following:

**HAIR.** Even though I groom myself regularly, routine brushing is needed. Brushing distributes my skin oil, reduces parasites and removes dead hair. Start with <u>very</u> short grooming sessions, stroking and brushing small areas each time until I become accustomed to the idea. If my tail starts to twitch or my ears flatten backwards against my head, discontinue the grooming session. Brushing two or three times a week is necessary if I am a long-haired cat and <u>daily</u> if I am a Persian cat. Brushing me once a week is usually sufficient if I am a short-haired cat. Purchase good quality grooming equipment. A rubber curry brush, a slicker brush and a natural short-bristle brush are needed for short hair. A slicker brush, a wide-toothed metal comb and a natural long-bristle brush are needed for long-hair. If needed, a soft toothbrush can be used to groom my face. Consult my veterinarian or a pet supply store concerning my grooming tools.

**TABBY TIP:**

Cats devote 1/3 of their waking hours to grooming.

When brushing me, place me in your lap or on a surface that is not wobbly or slippery. If I am a short-haired cat, first remove dead hair by massaging my torso with a rubber curry brush. Use a circular motion. Next, brush my hair with a slicker brush in the direction my coat lies. Finish with a bristle brush to smooth my hair. If I am a long-haired cat, first use a slicker brush to loosen dead hair. Brush the hair from my tail base toward my head and then brush my underbelly, behind my ears and under my legs to prevent mats. Next, comb through my hair with a wide-toothed stainless steel comb with blunt tips. Finish with a bristle brush to smooth my hair, brushing from my head toward my tail base. If there are mats that cannot be combed out, try untangling a small section at a time with your fingers or consider purchasing a mat remover at a pet store. Mat removers are usually safer than using scissors. Do not bathe me because water tightens the mats. If the mats are severe, my veterinarian may have to shave the area or I may require professional grooming. Make sure the groomer maintains a clean and secure facility. A reputable groomer requires proof of inoculations prior to grooming me and provides references. Do not use a groomer who suggests tranquilizing me before grooming. Some groomers are willing to make house calls.

My skin is a good barometer of my general health, so check it for irritation, lumps, or external parasites while brushing me. (See PAWS to consider/EXTERNAL PARASITES, page 56.) When a problem is found, the earlier it is treated by my veterinarian, the easier it is to cure.

When I am an adult, brushing regularly helps to reduce the likelihood of hairballs which can become a serious problem. Usually, I cough up the hairball or it is passed through the intestines. However, if I am unable to pass the hairball, I may vomit after eating; cough or gag excessively; stop eating; or become constipated. Consult my veterinarian if any of these events occurs. A preventive gel is available that aids in the passage of ingested hair.

48

It is easy to administer and I will probably like the taste. Mineral oil or petroleum jelly are not safe treatments. Occasionally, a hairball must be surgically removed. Several adult cat foods and treats are available to help control the formation of hairballs.

**EYES.** My eyes should be bright and clear. Should you notice a dried discharge in the corner of an eye, use a sterile pad or washcloth dipped in warm water to clean the area. Wipe my eyes in the direction of my nose and away from my ears. If I am Persian, wipe the folds under my eyes daily. For excessive tearing or discharge, take me to my veterinarian.

**EARS.** My ears should be checked regularly for ear mites or dirt. Dirt can be gently removed with a sterile pad and feline ear cleaning solution. Squirt the solution onto the pad and never directly into my ears. Clean only the visible area. Never penetrate the ear. Signs of mites include shaking my head or pawing at my ears. A dark, waxy discharge may be present. If you suspect mites, it is essential to take me to my veterinarian. Ear mites are common in kittens.

**WHISKERS.** My whiskers are my radar at night and a guide through tight areas. My whiskers should never be trimmed.

## YOUR HANDS

Your hands in daily grooming help my hair stay neat and clean;
Your hands that hold and brush me give my coat a healthy sheen.

Your hands perform great wonders when accompanied by praise.
Your hands can work to build a bond of trust in many ways.

Your hands are used to teach me and to make my training fun;
Your hands can offer me a treat for every task
    well done.

Your hands can throw a toy that I will
    eagerly pursue;
Your hands in gentle stroking say
    all good things come from you.

Your hands can scratch behind my ears
    when you return from work;
Your hands will give me loving care when I am sick or hurt.

Your hands are used with lots of love, but not to spank or shake.
Your hands will be a blessing so our bond of trust won't break!

# PHOTOS OF HANDS CARING FOR ME

# MORE PAWS

*Meouch!*

**PETicures.** This can be an intimidating project, and I will do everything possible to further your intimidation because I would rather make friends with the neighborhood dog than have my claws trimmed. I will wiggle, growl, bite, cry, and give you the dirtiest looks you have ever seen! If I would cooperate, the claw trimming would take approximately two minutes.

Cats generally do not like to have their feet held or handled. Every time you pet me, take a few minutes to caress or hold my feet. Let me get used to this idea before we ever tackle the task of trimming my claws. When we visit the veterinarian, ask him to demonstrate claw trimming and show you the quick in my claw, which is the pink or red vein inside the claw (see illustration). Have him check to see if I have dewclaws (located on the inside of each leg) that must be trimmed. The dewclaws can curl and grow inward causing lameness. Ask the veterinarian how often you need to trim my claws. Overgrown claws may cause foot problems or catch on carpeting or upholstery. You can use claw trimmers designed for cats or nail trimmers designed for humans. Purchase styptic powder in case you accidentally cut the vein in my claw.

BLOOD
NERVE

It is best to trim my claws just before my nap time when I am more relaxed. First, gather all supplies and then place me on a sturdy surface that is at a comfortable height for you. Another method is to roll me up securely in a towel and place me in your lap. Then, gently remove one paw at a time from the towel to trim the claws. Start the procedure by talking to me in a calm voice. To unsheathe the claw, take hold of my paw and gently press the large soft pad on the underside between your thumb and forefinger. Trim the clear, hooked part, avoiding the quick. If you should accidentally cut the quick, do not panic. The bleeding will not last long. Apply pressure and a small amount of styptic powder, ice, or cornstarch to the end of my nail to stop the bleeding. Give me plenty of love, and promise never to do it again! I will forgive you and promptly forget it. However, at this point, it may be better to discontinue the trimming until another day. If I struggle too much, trim only one paw and continue the next day. I will eventually get used to the procedure. As an indoor cat, I do not need my claws to defend myself. Therefore, trimming my claws regularly will help to protect your furniture. If claw trimming is not for you, take me to the veterinarian or groomer for this task.

### TABBY TIP:

My Paws and Claws

Lash out to defend
Knead to show contentment
Scratch to leave my scent
Stroke to show love
Rub my ear or face to indicate pain
Pat your cheek to say, "It's time to wake up!"

Check my paws occasionally for cuts or for small sharp objects that may have penetrated them. Limping or excessive licking of my paws may indicate that I have a problem. When a superficial wound is found, wash the area with warm water and apply an antiseptic. For a deep wound, take me to my veterinarian. If I should suddenly react negatively after I am accustomed to claw trimming, check my paws for an infection or embedded foreign object. Call my veterinarian, if necessary.

# FURTHER PAWS

**DENTAL HYGIENE.** Cats seldom have cavities, but they are prone to gum disease. Good dental hygiene should be established early. I will teethe between three and six months of age. If my baby teeth do not come out naturally, they must be extracted by my veterinarian. My need to chew becomes incessant during my teething period. Give me items that are safe to chew. Eating dry food may be painful while I am teething. If I seem to have a problem, moisten my dry food during this period. I may become fussy, have loose stool, or be lethargic while teething. My veterinarian can prescribe a topical ointment which is applied to my gums to alleviate teething pain. Similar products made for humans are toxic to cats.

After my permanent teeth are in place, resume my regular eating habits. Eating soft foods and table scraps will cause me to develop tartar buildup earlier than if I am eating a balanced dry feline diet. Dry food aids in scraping the teeth so tartar cannot form. Tartar control treats are also available. Prevent tartar build-up at the gumline by brushing my teeth with a feline toothpaste and a feline toothbrush. Cleaning pads that are used with oral cleaning solutions are also available for cats. Before using feline dental products, read the instructions. Do not use toothpaste meant for humans because it can irritate my gastrointestinal tract.

To introduce me to tooth brushing, spread a little feline toothpaste on my toothbrush and let me lick it. Gradually introduce the brush to the inside of my mouth. Gently lift my lip and insert the brush between the inside of my cheek and my teeth. Using a circular motion, brush a few teeth, or one side of my mouth one day and the other the next. When you have finished, give me lots of praise. Brushing my teeth twice a week should be sufficient.

My dental care should start early. If it was not possible and you suspect periodontal disease, take me to my veterinarian for a check-up. Signs of periodontal disease include:

- tartar build-up and the presence of pus
- discolored teeth
- swollen, red, inflamed, sore, or softened gum tissue
- head shaking
- loose or missing teeth
- loss of appetite
- bad breath
- salivating excessively
- pawing my face

Periodontal disease can lead to infection resulting in tooth loss and other complications, such as heart, liver or kidney problems. Pale gums may be a sign of poor health. Even with conscientious dental care, professional teeth cleaning may be needed occasionally. Consult my veterinarian about how often cleaning is required.

## THE IZE HAVE IT!

Nobility of spirit is a trait cats symbolize;
We walk in grace and beauty which our people glamorize!

They verbalize our antics 'til the tales are over-sized.
They think of us as more than cats . . . We're people in disguise!

We're fantasized, romanticized; we're idolized and socialized;
We're humanized and energized; we've also been mythologized!

We're maximized and  highly prized.  Our people recognize
That cats can be devoted friends, although we're just pint-sized!

The creature comforts of our lives we'd <u>never</u> jeopardize . . .
We love to live the pampered life . . . Now, <u>that</u> is paradise!!!

PHOTOS OF ME LOOKING MY BEST

53

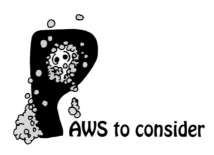

## PAWS to consider

**BATHING.** Brushing me regularly eliminates the need for a bath. This is good news because water and cats are not an ideal match. Occasionally, bathing may be necessary to remove excessive oil from my hair; to rid my body of fleas; to remove soil from my coat; or to clear up a skin disorder. If I have dandruff or excessively oily hair, I may need a change of diet. I should not be wet-bathed if I am under six months of age, ill, pregnant or when suffering from problems related to old age. Under these circumstances, use a dry shampoo which is sold at pet stores or veterinary offices.

**TABBY TIP:**
A smart cat "parent" trims the cat's claws before giving it a bath!

When a water bath is necessary, it is wise to have an assistant. Cover yourself with a long, durable, plastic apron. Assemble all supplies beforehand. You will need a small washcloth to clean my face and several towels — two for me and, at least two for you. Place a plastic pan in a small sink or a laundry tub. The area should be warm and draft free. Before bathing me, close the door to the bathing area to prevent my escape. (A soapy cat is impossible to catch!) Place a towel or rubber mat in the pan so I will feel secure. Brush my hair first. Place a cotton ball in each ear and a small amount of mineral oil in the corner of each eye. The oil prevents irritation should shampoo get into my eyes. Use feline shampoo. Shampoos made for dogs and humans do not have the correct PH balance for my skin.

Work quickly! Talk to me in a calm voice throughout the bath. Wash my face and ears with the small cloth using lukewarm water without shampoo. You do not want to get shampoo into my eyes or mouth. Next, wet my hair with lukewarm water. A spray attachment or a bowl of water with a cup is helpful. When using a spray attachment, hold it close to my body so that the spray will not frighten me. Working from my head back, apply a small amount of the cat shampoo. Massage shampoo throughout my hair. Then rinse very thoroughly. Do not leave shampoo residue which can irritate my skin. After I am rinsed, wrap a towel around me and pat me dry. Rubbing too much can tangle my hair, causing mats. It is very important that I am not chilled. If you cannot towel dry me completely, place me in my carrier and put me in a warm area until I am dry. If I will tolerate it, use a hair dryer on the lowest setting to dry my hair. After I am dry, brush my hair once more and give me a treat and lots of love. I may be angry with you but be patient; I will come around.

Be alert for a condition known as 'stud tail' which appears as crusty or greasy deposits at the base of my tail. Stud tail occurs when a gland on the upper side of the tail secretes too much oil. Stud tail can be spot cleaned, so ask my veterinarian for product recommendations. This condition is found more often in un-neutered males, although it can occur in females and neutered males. Diarrhea may leave dried feces around my anal area. Keep the area around my tail clean, but if diarrhea persists, consult my veterinarian. When feces stick to my hair after defecation, trim the hair in that area.

At any age I may develop feline acne on my chin. The acne, resembling blackheads, may result from an allergy to plastic bowls, or from an undetermined cause. Treatment is available from my veterinarian.

54

PHOTOS OF ME BEING BATHED OR BATHING MYSELF

**P**AWS to consider

**EXTERNAL PARASITES.** The most common external parasites that plague even an indoor cat are fleas and mites. These feed on my blood while living on my skin and inside my ears. Cleaning my bedding often and brushing my coat regularly will minimize parasitic infestations.

**FLEAS.** Fleas can cause anemia and — in rare cases — death. They can transmit tapeworm and cause severe flea allergy dermatitis. Excessive scratching; biting my body; or displaying bald spots or scabby sores; may be signs that I have fleas. If you suspect fleas, comb my hair with a flea comb. The comb removes fleas and flea dirt (the digested blood excreted by the fleas). Flea dirt resembles ground pepper.

To get rid of these tenacious pests you should quickly and aggressively battle them on three fronts: our <u>home</u>, my <u>bedding</u>, and <u>me</u>. Consult my veterinarian for effective and safe products. To maximize the flea kill, thoroughly vacuum all carpets and rugs, throwing away the vacuum bag. Treat our home with an insecticide. Do not allow me access to treated areas until they are completely dry. If the flea infestation is severe, contact a professional extermination service. Bathe me with a good feline flea control shampoo. Shampoos made for dogs can be deadly for me. Make a thick lather around my neck to prevent fleas from running into my ears or nose because fleas in these areas are much harder to treat. To be effective, the shampoo should soak my coat for ten minutes. Always take care to keep the shampoo away from my eyes. Sprays and powders are available and easier than a bath. Spray the solution onto a cotton ball; then wipe it over my dry hair. Use products intended just for cats and only one product at a time, unless, my veterinarian recommends otherwise. Read product instructions very carefully before using. If I need further treatment, take me to my veterinarian or groomer for a flea dip.

If you intend to purchase a flea collar for me, be aware of the following precautions:

- Do not use a flea collar before I am three months of age.
- Let the flea collar air out for twenty-four hours before using it the first time.
- Check under my collar frequently for an allergic reaction.
- Do not allow me to wear the flea collar to bed or in an enclosed space.
- Never let me chew my flea collar because it is toxic.
- Use a feline flea collar. Canine flea collars are toxic to cats.

The authors recommend a topical flea control product, such as Advantage® or Frontline® Plus. These products are prescribed by my veterinarian. Both are effective even after exposure to water. Advantage® can be used on kittens at 8 weeks and Frontline® Plus at 12 weeks of age. Both are applied monthly to the skin. The solution spreads naturally throughout the skin surface at the hair follicle as the pet moves. Over-the-counter topical flea products are not always effective. <u>Read the instructions and warning labels carefully</u>.

**LICE.** Few cats have lice. However, if I am scratching and biting my fur continuously, lice may be the problem. Lice are difficult to see. Sometimes the nits (eggs that the female lays on the hair shaft) can be seen. A severe infestation of lice can leave me weak from blood loss. The treatment for lice is similar to flea treatment. Consult my veterinarian about the use of powders, dips, or insecticide sprays.

**MITES.** Mites are transmitted to me from other infested animals. Mites, which are barely visible, can cause mange, skin lesions, infections, and even death. Ear mites are responsible for serious ear infections and, when present, cause me to excessively scratch my ears. I may cry and squeal when I scratch. The discomfort may cause me to tilt my head to one side when walking. If you notice sores around my ears; a dark brown wax inside my ear; or a foul smell in my ear canal; the problem could be ear mites. Mites may be transmitted to humans. If you suspect mites, consult my veterinarian about a preventative.

**RINGWORM.** Ringworm is a fungus, not a worm. Symptoms of ringworm are loss of hair in the infected areas, and patches of dry, scaly skin that continue to enlarge as the disease spreads. It is treated by shaving the infected hair, applying a fungicidal ointment, and giving oral doses of Griseofulvin. Ringworm is contagious to other animals and humans. Consult my veterinarian for treatment. It may be necessary to sterilize or destroy my toys, collar, and bedding.

**TICKS.** Luckily, tick-related problems are rare for cats since cats remove ticks through grooming before the tick can transmit a disease. Ticks are responsible for severe infections, such as Lyme disease and Rocky Mountain Spotted Fever. The tick which causes Lyme disease is so small that it is difficult to see. If I am at risk for Lyme disease, ask my veterinarian about the Lyme vaccine. The clinical symptoms of Lyme disease are lethargy, fever, depression, arthritis, sudden onset of severe pain, lameness, or loss of appetite. The clinical symptoms for Rocky Mountain Spotted Fever are high fever, decreased appetite, depression, enlarged lymph nodes, dehydration, weight loss, possible swelling of the legs and lower abdomen, and hemorrhaging from tissues of the mouth. If I exhibit any of these symptoms, take me to my veterinarian immediately. When I am allowed outdoors in warm weather, check often for ticks, including my ears and between my toes.

When a tick is found, you will need to remove it. Feline-safe tick insecticides can be applied directly to the tick. They kill the tick, causing it to release its hold on me. Another effective tick removal method is the use of tweezers. Hold the tweezers against the skin and remove the whole tick by pulling it straight out and destroying it. The tick's head is quite small and must be removed or it can cause an infection.

After removal, apply an antiseptic to the bite area. Should it be necessary to take me to the veterinarian, put the tick in a plastic bag and take it with you. A tick can infect you, too, so do not handle it with your bare hands. If we live in an area where ticks are numerous, clear my yard of weeds and tall grasses. Better yet, keep me indoors.

# THE ITCH

We cats, regardless of our breed,
Are set upon by parasites;
On us they simply love to feed,
Those pesky fleas and ticks and mites.

We claw and paw and scratch and bite;
The itch does not seem fittin'!
We're not immune, so it's a plight,
For every cat and kitten.

Apply a little pesticide,
From ear tips to our fannies;
There'll be no place for pests to hide,
On Fluffies, Sams, and Annies!

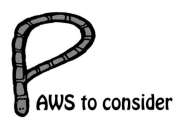

# AWS to consider

**INTERNAL PARASITES.** The most common internal parasites are coccidia, giardia, flukes, heartworm, hookworm, roundworm, tapeworm, and whipworm. Most of these parasites live in my intestines; although the heartworm, in its adult stage, lives in my heart and blocks the blood flow. During my first year, I need to be tested often for internal parasites. As an adult cat, I should be tested once a year or if I exhibit symptoms. Scooting my bottom on the ground is generally not a symptom of worms, but of impacted anal glands which require veterinary attention. Internal parasites should be treated by my veterinarian, because over-the-counter products are generally ineffective. Many of these parasites can be avoided by keeping me indoors.

**COCCIDIA AND GIARDIA.** These organisms are contracted by drinking contaminated water. They live in the intestine and are transferred from cat to cat through feces. Both cause diarrhea, weakness, and emaciation.

**FLUKES.** These parasites are contracted when a cat eats raw fish or kills and eats small infested animals. The parasite infects the liver, lungs or small intestines. My veterinarian can detect flukes by examining my fecal sample or respiratory secretions.

**HEARTWORM.** Heartworm is the most dangerous parasite, but luckily, is preventable. It is transmitted from an infected cat to me through mosquito bites. Unfortunately, symptoms may not present themselves until it is too late to save me. Symptoms of heartworm include coughing, fatigue, labored breathing, and extreme weakness. A blood sample can be checked for evidence of heartworm. Treatment options will be discussed if heartworm is present. Thereafter, I will require yearly testing.

**HOOKWORM.** Hookworm can cause anemia and severe intestinal problems. I can be infected with hookworm through skin penetration or by ingesting the fecal matter of another cat. Hookworm symptoms include bloody stool, pale gums and emaciation.

**ROUNDWORM.** Roundworm is the most common internal parasite of cats and can be passed to me from my mother. They resemble pieces of spaghetti, and are visible in my feces. My fecal sample should be tested during my first visit to my veterinarian. Signs of roundworm include worms or mucus in the feces, diarrhea, a dull coat, coughing or a pot-bellied appearance. Roundworm can be transmitted to humans.

**TAPEWORM.** Tapeworms live and consume digested food in my intestines. I contract them by eating infected fleas or rodents. The symptoms include diarrhea, emaciation, or a dull brittle coat. Check my stool and around the anus for white rice-like segments.

**WHIPWORM.** Whipworms live in my large intestine. I may have no symptoms, or I may develop diarrhea, dehydration, or weight loss. Whipworms are found throughout the United States and are difficult to eradicate. I contract them by ingesting feces containing whipworm eggs.

With the exception of heartworm, worms can be detected by a fecal exam.

# PURRsonals

When my "parent(s)" comes home, I greet him/her by_____

_____

My "parent(s)" greets me by _____

When visitors come, I rub against them_____, hide_____,

beg for attention _____, cuddle up on the lap of the only one who dislikes

cats _____, or _____

I show affection to my "parent(s)" by  head bumps _____, rubbing against

his/her legs _____, or _____

When I see another cat, I _____

When I see a dog, I _____

I am learning to use my scratching post, but I still like to claw the _____

_____

I was in big trouble when I clawed or chewed _____

I tore up the _____

I usually use my litter box, but once, I decided to use the flower pot.   Yes/No   (circle one).

or I used the  _____

When I did, my "parent(s)" did the following to prevent me from using it again: _____

_____

I use my paw to bat _____

The cutest thing I do is _____

_____

The smartest things I do are _____

I get a treat whenever I _____

FOUR TO FIVE MONTHS

61

I weigh _____. I am _____ tall.

This month I've learned: _____

_____

I visited my veterinarian on _____
(I need more inoculations between four and five months)

I was given the following shots: _____

_____

My veterinarian said that I was _____

I was checked for parasites. I had none _____ or I had the following parasites: _____

_____

My veterinarian gave me the following medicine to take home: _____

_____

When my exam was finished my veterinarian gave me_____

_____

While I was at the veterinarian's office I was relaxed _____, hissed _____,

shook _____, complained _____, or _____

_____

My "parent(s)" calmed me by _____

At home, I took my medicine in my _____, on my _____,

with a _____, stuffed inside a _____

I spit it out (Yes/No), swallowed it whole (Yes/No), clamped my mouth shut (Yes/No),

never noticed it (Yes/No). (Circle one.)

(See Some PURRfectly Good Advice/ADMINISTERING MEDICINE, page 110.)

## PAWS to consider

**TRAINING.** When I am well-trained, my good behavior will be a credit to you. Through training, I should become willingly obedient. Training is important for my safety and sociability.

Almost any mammal will respond to training when food treats are used as an inducement. When praise is included, you have a winning combination for a successful training program. Treats and praise create an atmosphere of positive reinforcement that work wonders with cats. The key to a satisfactory result is to give the treat and praise <u>after</u> I have performed the desired behavior. Never use physical punishment because I will not understand. I will fear you and resort to undesirable behavior when you are not around. Always use remote punishment, such as a water gun or a plant sprayer set on "stream". Loud noises or compressed air are excellent corrections when used in a timely manner. These methods will be incorporated into the following text when appropriate.

**INDOOR TRAINING.** This training is being addressed first because it is the most important. Besides having a safe and happy cat, you will have the satisfaction of knowing that I am not invading the property of others, where I may catch and kill healthy songbirds, or contaminate or destroy a garden. Our neighbors will appreciate your consideration. If you adopted me as a kitten, indoor training should not be difficult. Allow me outdoors <u>only</u> when I am on a leash and harness or in a safe cat enclosure.

If you have any doubt about the value of indoor training, please read the following comparison.

| Indoor Cat | Outdoor Cat |
|---|---|
| Lives 12-20 years: Has only slight exposure to disease | Lives only 1-5 years: Is exposed to leukemia, kitty AIDS and parasites that can be transmitted to humans |
| Cannot be attacked by stray cats, dogs, or other predatory animals | Can be attacked, maimed, or killed |
| Is not endangered by animal traps | Can be caught in leg hold traps |
| Cannot suffer from frostbite | Can be exposed to severe weather |
| Cannot be hit by cars | Can be hit by cars |
| Cannot become lost and cannot go hungry | Can become lost and die from starvation |
| Cannot be abused | Can be abused |
| Is safe from toxic materials | Can be poisoned or shot by hunters |

**You decide!**

If I was an outdoor cat before you adopted me, training me to stay indoors may be tedious but not impossible. It takes about four to six weeks to retrain me. Be <u>very</u> observant whenever the door is opened. During the retraining period, I may be stressed and perform a few acts that you will not like, such as failing to use the litter box. If you need advice during this period, consider contacting the Tree House Animal Foundation in Chicago at (773) 784-5488 or www.treehouseanimals.org; or contact Cats International at (262) 375-8852 or www.catsinternational.org. As I adjust to the new routine, reward me with treats and praise. Cats are creatures of habit and the outdoors can be filled with alluring adventures. To change my habits, provide interesting indoor activities, such as a scratching post, a quiet place to take a nap and play periods with hunting-type games. When you return home, I may try to dash out the door as soon as it is opened. Keep a squirt gun outside by the door. Open the door slowly and, if I try to escape, squirt me. Do not let me see you squirt the water. Make it look like the door is doing this. If loud noises frighten me, try rolling a tin can filled with coins through the doorway as it opens or drop your keys, purse, or briefcase. Should I escape, get a treat and call my name. When I return, give me the treat, lots of praise and then take me indoors. Next time, try to be more alert. Outdoor cat enclosure kits are available for cats that enjoy being outdoors. (See Some PURRfectly Good Advice/ CAT ENCLOSURE KITS, page 111.) These enclosures allow a cat to be outdoors in a safe environment. A cat should not be placed outdoors in extreme or wet weather or left outdoors when no one is home.

CARRIER TRAINING. It is important that I adapt to my carrier in preparation for the time when I will be transported by car. Set my carrier in a sunny spot and place my favorite treats about two feet in front of it. Let me investigate and eat the treats. Repeat for a week, but continue to move the treats closer to the carrier each day. The second week open the carrier door and secure it so it does not move. Place treats at the entrance of my carrier. Repeat for a week. The third week place a towel or blanket in the carrier and place the treats inside each day. Allow me to go in and out as I please. The fourth week place the treats inside the carrier. If I go into the carrier, close the door quietly and keep it closed for a few seconds. Then open the door. Repeat for the rest of the week. Each time I go into the carrier, praise me. After the fourth week, leave the carrier in the same place and put a favorite toy inside. Occasionally leave a treat, or spray the inside with catnip. When it is time to transport me by car, place a treat in the carrier, and then place me inside. If I still balk, stand the carrier on end with the open door on top. Lower me into the carrier hind feet first. Praise me and reassure me that all is well. It is not safe for me to be loose in a car. I can get under your feet while you are driving or be seriously hurt if you have to stop suddenly. While riding in a car, secure the carrier with one of the seatbelts. (Miss Flori has never adjusted to a carrier and meows excessively while inside one. However, for safety sake, she is always placed in one while in a car. Jodi uses a carrier that opens at the top and the side. The top opening is more convenient when placing Miss Flori inside the carrier or removing her from it.)

COME If you have been led to believe that I cannot be trained to come when called, then be prepared to give up that myth. Coming when called could save my life someday if I should escape the safety of my home, or if a fire or dangerous weather forces us to take shelter.

Begin my training by choosing a special sound that is not high pitched or irritating. Shaking a treat can or the sound of a small jingle bell are examples. Whatever object you choose to make your special sound should always be accessible. Start by calling me at mealtime. Remember to use the word "come" followed by my name and our special sound. Cats adore routine and ritual, so always feed me at the same time each day. Once I am routinely coming for meals, vary the activity and call me at other times. When I respond, give me a treat. By letting me take my treat from your hand, you have enabled me to view you as the source of all goodness. If practiced regularly for just five minutes a day, I will come when I hear your voice and our special sound.

(Miss Flori receives a few bites of chicken each day which is referred to as "chickie". When she is needed, all one has to do is call out, "Miss Flori, chickie"! She miraculously appears. Of course, if the word chickie is said, chickie must be delivered. There is one exception. Miss Flori lives in an area frequented by tornados. When the warning siren sounds, the dogs and Miss Flori are called and are expected to go to the basement. "Chickie" is given out after the emergency has passed.)

LEASH TRAINING. Walking in a harness and leash should be taught in preparation for trips to my veterinarian, a walk around our yard or accompanying you on vacation. Begin training me in our home in an area where I will not be easily distracted. Use an H-shaped harness — it is safer than a collar because I cannot wiggle out of it. A light-weight nylon or cotton leash is a must. Do not use a chain! It is too heavy for a cat. Let me inspect my harness and wear it around the house for a few hours before attaching the leash. When I walk in the harness and leash, reward me with a tasty treat. Do not reward me for lying down on the job or refusing to move. Continue to practice with me in our home. When I feel secure about walking in a harness and leash, go outdoors.

When going for a "walk", don't expect me to plod along beside you like a dog. I will not walk at a steady pace. Make our "walks" pleasant by following my lead. Be prepared to stop frequently. The key to introducing me to the leash is to let me think that I am leading you. A lead of no more than four to six feet will allow you to more easily keep me under control. Walk in peaceful, dog-free areas. If danger threatens, scoop me up, but do not be neurotic about it or I will become skittish. It may be several weeks before I allow you to actually lead me. If you are gentle and patient, I will accept leash walking as a natural part of living with people. Teaching me to walk using a harness and leash will prove invaluable for potty breaks during travel. (Miss Flori loathes any kind of restraint, so she goes outdoors for supervised play only in an area that is completely enclosed and safe.)

<u>OFF</u>. When training for the "off" command, be consistent. It will confuse me if you use "off" one time and "down" the next. The following training method requires treats; therefore, start the training when I am hungry. To teach me the "off" command, place me on an elevated structure. Place a treat in front of my nose and then slowly lower the treat to the floor, saying my name, followed by the word, "Off!". As soon as I jump down, give me the treat and lots of praise. Repeat this action several times for about five minutes. When I lose interest, stop the training, and start again the next day. Cats usually do not like to be forced to do anything. When I have mastered "off", you should be able to discontinue the treats and just issue the "off" command. Each time I am successful, praise me lavishly. I will enjoy the praise as much as a treat.

<u>PEOPLE FOOD</u>. The first time I jump onto the dinner table and snatch a morsel from your plate, it may be very cute. However, it is a habit that should be nipped in the bud or it will  become a nuisance. Before setting your food on the table, secure some cat treats. As soon as I jump onto the table, yell "No!" and stomp your feet on the floor. Most kitties do not like sudden loud noises. If I jump off the table, praise me and give me a treat. If I do not jump off  the table, say "Off!", place me on the floor and give me a treat. Initially, this action should be repeated as often as necessary until I catch on to what you want. Once I learn to stay off the table, reward me with a few cat treats after you finish dining. Feeding me at the same time you eat may keep me from being interested in your food.

<u>TRICKS</u>. You can teach me tricks, such as sit, down, fetch, and sit-up. The question is, "Why would I want to learn canine tricks when I come with my own phenomenal bag of cat tricks?" How many dogs do you know that can leap from a sitting position on the floor to the top of a fireplace mantel with little effort? How many can tear through the house ending with an airborne somersault? And how many can effortlessly assume various yoga positions; open doors; or climb straight up a wall or drapes with incredible agility? The bottom line is that dog tricks are boring to a cat. Let me show off my antics in my style and on my time. Just sit back and enjoy me!

No frisbee catchin',
Ball chasin',
Or beggin' for my food.
I'm an independent critter
With a spunky CATtitude!

# PURRfection!

All cats have their own PURRsonality,
As they walk through our lives with PURRpose.

No cat needs to strive for PURRfection,
At least not from the cat's PURRception.

The cat trains its people with PURRsistence,
And with a gentle type of PURRsuasion.

So, you see, from the cat's PURRspective,
A cat's PURRsona would give its people
**PURRfection!**

# PURRsonals

## THINGS MY CAT HAS TRAINED ME TO DO AND VICE VERSA

_____

_____

_____

_____

_____

_____

_____

_____

_____

_____

_____

_____

_____

_____

_____

_____

_____

68

# PAWS to consider

**BEHAVIORAL PROBLEMS.** At some time I may develop a behavioral problem. Because cats love routine and consistency, behavioral problems many times arise due to a change in my schedule or environment. To correct a bad habit, sometimes all that is needed is the timely use of the word "No!" or consistent attention to the problem. Addressing the problem one minute and looking the other way the next sends conflicting messages. Many cats are abandoned or given away because their owners did not take time to properly train or retrain them. It takes four to six weeks to change a pattern of behavior, so be patient. When training me, try to look at the world through my eyes. Positive training methods, such as the use of praise, food treats, or petting are most effective. Never resort to physical punishment. Using physical force is not a solution when training a cat. In fact, it makes the problem worse because I will think I am being attacked. My instinct will be to fight back or hide whenever I see you. If a problem has grown beyond your control, consult my veterinarian to make sure I do not have a physical condition; or consult a cat behaviorist. The Humane Society of the United States (HSUS) and the American Society for the Prevention of Cruelty to Animals (ASPCA) offer advice on behavioral problems. Visit their websites at www.hsus.org or www.aspca.org. For HSUS click on "pets", then "pet behavior" followed by "cat behavior". For ASPCA click on "pet care", then on "Animal training and behavior" and then on "cats". The following paragraphs list common behavioral problems and some problem-solving suggestions:

**Aggression/Biting.** Aggression is a part of my nature because I am a hunter. There are several types of aggression: defensive, irritable, play, sexual, and territorial. In <u>defensive aggression</u>, I am trying to protect myself. I am not my normal self and may consider you an added threat. At this time, it is best to leave me alone. Let me retreat and hide. When I am frightened, my pupils will dilate and I may hiss, growl, or flatten my body against the ground. My ears will flatten against my head. Try to remove whatever is frightening me. Once I have relaxed, talk to me softly and stroke me. If I am a nervous cat, having problems adjusting to my new home, consult my veterinarian.

I may exhibit <u>irritable aggression</u> when I am forced to do something I do not want to do; played with too roughly; or handled too long. If I lash my tail, stop what you are doing because it is irritating me and I may suddenly bite or scratch you. Do not resort to physical punishment if this should happen. You caused the problem. I am just reacting in a cat-like manner because I cannot verbally tell you to "Cut it out!". Usually, irritable aggression is mild and short-lived if the irritation is stopped.

Ambushing or ankle grabbing is part of <u>play aggression</u>. If I grab an ankle, stop moving. A stationary prey is not very interesting. A loud shriek followed by an equally loud "No!" can be effective in discouraging this type of play. Do not engage me in play after an attack or I will think that my aggressive actions are acceptable. When you are playing with me, do not allow me to play with your hands or feet because doing so encourages me to bite your fingers or toes. Biting may be cute when I am a kitty, but when I am fully grown, my bite will hurt. There are two ways that could curb play aggression: spend time playing with me or consider providing a feline companion. Direct my energy toward chase-and-pounce-type toys or stuffed toys filled with catnip. (See PAWS to consider/PLAY/EXERCISE, page 79.) Play periods should last at least ten minutes or until I am tired.

If I am spayed or neutered, <u>sexual aggression</u> should not be part of our lives. However, stroking the bellies of some cats can trigger sexual aggression. If I do not enjoy belly rubs, I will use my claws to convey the message and, undoubtedly, you will think twice before doing it again.

<u>Territorial aggression</u> can cause a great deal of misery for an outdoor, unneutered male. Males engage in territorial fights which can result in serious injuries. The solution is simple. Neuter me and keep me indoors unless supervised. (See PAWS to consider/TRAINING, page 62.) If I am marking my indoor territory with urine, see the section below on spraying. When there is more than one cat in the household, we will usually work out the pecking order ourselves. If one cat is causing harm to another, isolate the offender. Reintroduce the cats after a few days. Seek help from an animal behaviorist if the problem continues. There are medications for troublesome aggression. Sometimes aggression is caused by pain. When you suspect an illness or injury, consult my veterinarian. Keep in mind that, even though the play activity of some male cats is rough, they usually do not injure each other.

**Arrival of Baby.** Once a baby arrives keep my routine as consistent as possible and be sure to give me individual attention. I should be kept out of the baby's room. If I jump into the crib with the baby, I could accidentally lie on the baby's face, causing the child to suffocate. The baby and I should share only supervised time. In fact, all children should be supervised when they interact with me until they are old enough to assume some responsibility for my care. (See PAWS to consider/CHILDREN AND KITTIES, page 26.)

**Chewing My Fur.** Chewing my fur to the extent of causing hair loss means there is an underlying problem. I may have fleas, allergies, a fungus, or an infection. I may be suffering from stress. Consult my veterinarian and then, administer the proper medication. If stress is the problem, I may need short-term medication. Try to solve the problem that is causing the stress. When dogs or small children are in our home, establish a routine for me and safe places to retreat. Exercise, through play, will help to reduce my stress.

**Destructive Chewing.** I will lose my baby teeth between three and six months of age. During this time, chewing eases the pain as larger permanent teeth push out the baby teeth. I will chew anything I can get into my mouth; therefore, safety is a concern at this time. (See PAWS to consider/SAFETY, page 32.) Provide safe feline toys that I can chew. Spray feline repellent on furniture legs and other areas that I should not chew. Reapply the repellent every two days. When chewing is excessive, confine me to a smaller area during this period. When I am chewing due to stress, remove whatever is stressing me. When I am chewing because I am bored, provide extra play periods. Give me toys that will amuse me when I am alone. During this period, be sure to feed me on time. I may chew your possessions because I am hungry; therefore, increase my food allowance as I grow. (See PAWS to consider/FEEDING, page 38.)

**Destructive Scratching.** Scratching sharpens and cleans my claws by shedding their outer layers. To eliminate damage from scratching, trim my claws regularly and provide a scratching post. (See PAWS to consider/PETicures, page 50.) Scratching also releases stress and  marks my territory. Glands in my feet release a scent that tells other cats, "This is my space!". When I see the neighbor cat through a window, I will scratch the window sill to mark it as my territory. To discourage the neighbor's cat from visiting, spray it with water from the garden hose or install a Cat Fence-In™ barrier kit (888-738-9099). Cat Fence-In™ attaches to wood, masonry, wire, or chain link fences and keeps me safely fenced in — and stray cats out. If a bird feeder is attracting cats into our yard, removing it may solve the problem.

Good scratching post training can eliminate destructive scratching. Make one or two scratching posts available at all times. My scratching post should be sturdy; tall enough for a good stretch; and have a surface of sisal or carpet. Teach me to use the post by taking me to it and gently dragging my front feet down the surface. This marks the post with my scent. A scratching post placed by my sleeping area encourages use because most cats like a good stretch after sleeping. If the couch is my target, place the post in front of the couch. When you see me use the post, praise me lavishly and give me a treat. If I start to scratch the couch, redirect me to the post. Spraying or rubbing catnip on the post, or attaching a favorite toy may make the post more desirable. Placing a treat on top of the post works for some cats. Until I start using my scratching post, place double-sided tape or contact paper (sticky side up), or spray feline repellent on the damaged area. Most pet stores sell indoor feline repellent spray. Soft vinyl claw covers are available from my veterinarian. These cover the ends of my claws and protect household surfaces. Usually, the covers need to be replaced every four to six weeks. For information call Soft Paws® (800-433-7297).

Scratching is fundamental to my nature. This trait cannot be changed. A small number of cats cannot successfully be trained to use a scratching post consistently. If you have tried every remedy without success, consider declawing my front paws. It is far better to declaw them than to give me away or force me to live outdoors. It is not necessary to declaw the back claws. They usually do not cause damage and are needed for scratching myself, and for balance. Discuss this procedure with my veterinarian. Declawing should never be the first solution to a scratching problem. The surgery requires anesthesia and several days for recovery. Complications can include infection, pain and lameness. A veterinarian who uses a laser instead of a scalpel during the procedure lessens the healing time. After declawing, I must never be allowed outdoors unsupervised, because I cannot defend myself.

**Dislikes Being Handled.** I may not be a lap cat. I may be the type that likes to sit near you but not on you. Respect my wishes and do not force me to sit on your lap. To encourage me to interact with you, use praise and treats. Even if I am a lap cat, when I decide to leave your lap, let me go. Teach all members of the household the proper way to pick me up and carry me. (See PAWS to consider/CHILDREN, page 26). (Miss Flori was found and adopted as a stray when she was about ten months old. She has never adjusted to being a lap cat. However, if she discovers someone taking a nap, she loves to lie on that person's tummy. She then purrs loudly, which is a very pleasant sound when one is drifting off to sleep.)

**Finicky Eater.** Usually this problem is created by changing my diet too often. There is no need to change my food if I am eating the correct amount of nutritionally balanced cat food and am healthy and eliminating regularly. I do need a clean food bowl and fresh, clean water available every day. Unconsumed wet food should be thrown out before adding new food. Besides my regular food, give me a few treats each day. If it is necessary to change my food, do so gradually. Substitute twenty-five percent of my regular food with the new food. Every few days add a little more new food until it completely replaces the former food.

**Fearfulness.** If I am a shy kitty, allow me to approach visitors on my own terms. Give the visitor a treat that can be offered to me. I may prefer to retreat to a hiding place when visitors come, which is all right. We are not all social butterflies. In new situations, such as a trip to the veterinarian, I may become fearful; especially if I sense that you are upset. Therefore, take precautions that will protect me. Do not take offense if I strike out at you. I am just trying to protect myself.

**Hyperactivity.** Kittens have extremely high energy levels so what may seem hyper to you may be natural to me. Make my hyperactivity positive by playing with me every day for at least twenty minutes or by providing a companion kitten. When my nightly activity interferes with your sleep, confine me to my own room with my litter box and water bowl. Provide a climbing structure or perches and plenty of toys to keep me occupied. Feed me about one hour before bedtime. A full tummy may make me sleepy.

**Jumping onto Furniture or Counters.** Jumping is a natural instinct for a cat. If you try to curtail all my jumping you will have a neurotic cat. However, I can be trained to avoid jumping onto certain objects. The best way to stop me from jumping onto counters or furniture is to make the surface unpleasant to me. Cover a counter or table top with contact paper (sticky side up). When I jump onto the paper, I will not like the sticky substance on my paws. Pieces of plastic carpet runners (the kind with hard plastic "fingers" on the bottom) can be placed upside down on forbidden areas. When I jump onto the runner, I will not like the feel of hard plastic on my paws. Most cats do not like citrus odors. Placing a deodorizer with a citrus scent on the counter or table, may keep me away. Forbidden areas can be booby-trapped with tin cans filled with coins. Set the cans on the very edge of the counter so that, when I jump up, they will tumble to the floor. Usually the noise will scare me away. Teaching me the "off" command may be helpful. (See PAWS to consider/TRAINING, page 65.)

**Plant Eaters.** If I start to chew on your plants, spray them with Grannick's Bitter Apple ®. This product will not hurt the plants. Re-apply it every few days. Do not provide me with a kitty grass or catnip plant, which will only confuse me. I am not capable of differentiating between your plants and my plants, and will not understand why I cannot chew on both of them. Remove all poisonous plants from my area. (See SOME PURRfectly GOOD ADVICE, page 114, for a list of poisonous plants.)

**Raiding Trash.** Cats who love to eat may become trash can raiders. The easiest and most practical solution to the problem is to remove the trash can from my area by placing it under the sink or in a closet. If it is not possible, cover the trash can with a lid that I cannot pry off. Waste paper basket tippers can be discouraged by applying double-sided tape around the top edge of the basket. When I reach up to tip the basket, I will not like the feel of the tape on my paws.

**Separation Anxiety.** The stress of being left alone for long periods may cause me to become destructive. Until I am older, it is best to confine me to one room when you are away. Provide a litter box, food, water, and plenty of toys. To alleviate my boredom and anxiety during your absence, provide a window perch, a companion cat or consider hiring a pet sitter.

**Spraying.** Spraying is a cat's way of leaving a calling card. I am laying claim to you and the surrounding territory. Neutering or spaying usually solves the problem especially if I am neutered before sexually mature. Females also spray but not as often as males. Have me checked by my veterinarian to eliminate the possibility of a urinary tract infection which may be causing the problem.

Stressors that prompt me to spray are the following: moving to a new home; introducing a new object into our household; observing another cat through a window; bringing a new person or animal into the family; sudden loud noises. When moving to a new home, confine me to a safe area and then gradually admit me to the rest of the house. Keep a water gun handy. If I start to back up to an item with my tail raised, spray me with water but do not let me see you do it. Let me think it is the object that I intend to mark that is retaliating against me. An outdoor stimulus, such as, a neighborhood cat walking through our yard, can cause me to mark my territory. Either close the window covering or discourage the outdoor cat from our yard by spraying it with a garden hose. If yard items, such as bird feeders or baths, are attracting other cats to my yard, remove the items.

If I spray an area, clean the area by using an odor neutralizer formulated for feline urine. Feliway® is a product that, when sprayed on areas marked by urine, discourages future marking. Check out their web site at www.farnampet.com or ask my veterinarian about this product. If used on unmarked areas, it usually discourages me from marking those areas. Booby-trap areas by placing contact paper (sticky side up) on the floor in front of marked objects or consider closing off the room. Sometimes, placing my food bowl in an area where I spray discourages me from spraying that area again. If these suggestions fail, ask my veterinarian about hormonal or anti-stress medication that controls spraying. Exercise through play can relieve my stress.

**Suckling.** If I was taken from my mother at too early an age, I may develop the habit of sucking on my paws, your clothing, blankets, or other pets. When this behavior is a reaction to stress, resolve the stress. Buy me an artificial lambskin toy to suck. Whenever I start to suck or chew an unacceptable object, replace it with my lambskin toy. Praise me if I interact with the toy. Spray feline repellent on blankets or objects I am sucking or remove them from my reach until I outgrow the urge to suck.

**Urinating or Defecating Outside the Litter Box.** If I start soiling outside of the litter box, one of the following may be the reason.

1. My litter box is too dirty.
2. There are not enough litter boxes for the number of cats in our household.
3. My litter box is not conveniently located.
4. My litter box is in a public area instead of a quiet private area.
5. My litter box is too small for my size.
6. My litter is not to my liking.
7. My routine is upset and I am experiencing stress.
8. I have a medical problem.
9. My elimination timing is off because I am still a baby.
10. I am being intimidated by a dominate tom or queen.

There are solutions to all of these problems, but it takes commitment on your part. The first five problems are relatively easy to correct.

1. Cats do not like smelly, dirty litter boxes. My feces should be removed daily from my litter box. If clumping litter is used, all clumps should also be removed every day. Once the litter is clean, smooth out the area. Thoroughly clean the box once a week with warm water and soap. Then change the litter. When cleaning the box, do not use strong smelling cleaning agents because most cats are repelled by strong scents. If I am particularly finicky, you may have to change the litter every day.

2. In a household with more than one cat, a litter box should be provided for each cat. In multi-level homes, a litter box should be placed on each level.

3. My litter box should be accessible at all times. If I cannot find it or get to it, I cannot use it.

4. Litter boxes should be placed in quiet and private areas of the house. I do not like to be disturbed while using the litter box or ambushed my another cat or the resident canine. Put yourself in my paws. You would not want someone bursting into the bath room when you are using it! If I am frightened while using a litter box, I may not return to that particular box. Move that litter box to a new location that is safe and private. If I seek out a private area, such as behind a couch, I may prefer a covered litter box. While I am adjusting to a covered litter box, block off the areas you do not want me to use or cover them with double-sided tape.

5. The litter box should be appropriate for my size. The box is too small if I am defecating over the side. Solve the problem by buying a wider box with higher sides. I should be able to turn around in the box and have plenty of room for scratching to cover my stool and urine.

6. Experiment with various types of litter until you get it right. Do not use scented litter because most cats do not like it. Some even develop allergies to the scent. If I do not scratch in the litter or shake my paws after leaving the box, I probably do not like the litter you have chosen. Some cats will not use a box with a liner. Adjusting the depth of the litter may also solve the problem. You may be putting too much or too little in the box. One inch of litter is sufficient for small cats and two inches for large cats. (It took three types of litter and two kinds of litter boxes until Jodi got it right for Miss Flori. Until the problem was resolved, Miss Flori was using the living room carpet which did not fit in with Jodi's decor. Jodi installed two Scat Mats® at the threshold to the living room. When Miss Flori came into contact with these mats, she received safe, but uncomfortable, electrostatic pulses. This was enough to keep Miss Flori away from the living room. About eight months later, one of her cousin cats was visiting and taught Miss Flori how to use feline dexterity to circumvent the mats. By then, the habit of using the living room was forgotten. She was using her litter boxes regularly, so the mats were put away. For more information about Scat Mat®, call 800-767-8658 or visit their website at www.scatmat.com.)

7. Stress is a big factor concerning litter box problems. I can become stressed when we have moved; a baby has just arrived; a dog or other pet has been added to the household; I have been declawed; you are redecorating; or a member of the family has moved away. I dislike change so rearranging my schedule can also stress me. It takes time for me to adjust to change. While I am adjusting I may have accidents. Try to ease the stress by giving me extra attention and exercise.

8. A medical problem, such as a urinary tract infection or constipation, can cause litter box problems. If I experience pain while using the litter box, I will blame the box and not want to use it again. When you suspect a urinary tract infection, take me to the veterinarian immediately as this is <u>very</u> serious. Constipation may require a diet change. Consult my veterinarian.

9. When I am young, I may wait until the last minute to use the litter box and sometimes I will not make it. The problem should disappear as I mature. (When Miss Flori was young, she would occasionally break all Olympic track records while racing through the kitchen to the laundry room litter box. As she matured, she eventually learned the value of being in the right place at the right time.)

10. In a multi-cat family, having more than one litter box, eliminates competition for the box. Usually, cats in the same household that have been spayed or neutered establish relatively harmonious relationships. However, if one cat is causing problems for the others, and you are unable to correct the problem, isolate the offending cat or consult an animal behaviorist.

Once you have found the right type of litter box and litter and the best location, do not change anything! If I have an accident outside the litter box, and you catch me in the act, yell "No!" Pick me up and take me to my litter box immediately. Should I run away from the tone of your voice, do not chase me, or I may continue to urinate from fear. Always clean the spot with feline odor neutralizer. Even if you cannot detect an odor, I can. Do not use an ammonia-based product for cleaning because ammonia is a component of urine. The odor of the ammonia will attract me back to that area. Cover the area for a few days. One of our veterinarian consultants, recommends placing a plastic carpet runner (the kind with hard plastic "fingers" on the bottom) over the area. Place the runner upside down. Cats do not like the feel of hard plastic on their paws. This material is inexpensive and washable. If I am using a potted plant as a litter box, cover the soil with double-sided tape in a crisscrossed pattern or use chicken wire.

Yowling. Some cats speak very little while others, such as the Siamese, speak frequently and loudly. When I yowl because you did not attend to my needs, take care of the matter. When I yowl for no apparent reason, try to change my behavior by ignoring or distracting me. Start playing with me and I will forget my original demand. This might be a good time to place me and a ping-pong ball in the bathtub. Try to remember to praise me when I am quiet. Give me a treat and tell me how good I am. If my vocalizing is excessive, mild anti-anxiety medication may be needed. If I just like to talk to you, enter into a conversation with me, but do not give in to my demands unless they are reasonable. Do not worry about appearing foolish. People talk to their cats. You are just one of the lucky ones who has a cat that answers.

## CAT CHAT

The happy cat that feels secure is an aristocrat.
It greets the world with grace and style that says, "Hi, I'm a cat!"

Beware the cat with sideways stance, arched back and bristled hair.
Its posture shows hostility; its eyes an angry glare!

The timid cat feels insecure displaying twitching tail,
It demonstrates uncertainty; may hide or flee or wail!

The laid-back cat is napping for there's not a thing to prove.
It takes a cataclysmic force to make that kitty move!

Each cat whatever size and breed, from time to time may be,
Depending on the circumstance, each of these types you see!

PHOTOS OF ME WITH AN ATTITUDE

PHOTOS OF ME WITH AN ATTITUDE

# FIVE TO SIX MONTHS

I weigh _____. I am _____tall.

This month I've learned: _____

_____

My "parent(s)" describes my personality as _____

I am happy when _____

I am unhappy when _____

I saw my reflection in _____

I love it when someone scratches my _____

I tolerate _____

I use my tail to indicate _____

_____

I respond to loud noises by _____

When I am afraid, I arch my back and growl _____, run and hide _____,

meow loudly _____, or _____

My "parent(s)" comforts me by _____

I am afraid of:

_____ thunder

_____ fireworks

_____ loud noises

_____ vacuum cleaners

I am not afraid of anything, but I do not like _____

I threw a temper tantrum when _____because _____

_____

# PURRsonals

I like to play with _____

My favorite floppy toys are _____

_____

My favorite toys that roll are _____

_____

My favorite crackly toys are _____

_____

When a fly or small insect catches my attention, I _____

When I catch an insect in the house, I _____

My favorite activities to do with my "parent(s)" are _____

_____

I try to engage my "parent(s)" in play by _____

_____

I amuse myself by _____

_____

I can carry _____ in my mouth

I like to hide my toys in _____

I like to play in water dripping at the sink.  Yes/No  (circle one).

My "parent(s)" taught me the following tricks: _____

_____

When I finish playing, my favorite place to take a cat nap is _____

_____

At night, while others are trying to sleep, I _____

_____

**P**AWS to consider

PLAY/EXERCISE. We kitties are lucky. We never worry about our inner thighs, our bustlines, or our sagging bottoms. If fed and exercised properly, we should not have a weight problem. However a steady stream of human treats and lying on the couch watching the "Aristocats" will put us at the same risk as humans. Fat cats are uncomfortable and definitely unhealthy. Excessive weight can cause heart, digestive, respiratory and hip problems. If I have difficulty grooming myself, moving about or have built up fat around my middle or haunches, I am overweight. If you think that I have developed a weight or health problem, consult my veterinarian about diet changes, exercise and feeding habits.

I need at least fifteen minutes of vigorous exercise a day. Exercise will continue to build a bond between us, relax me, help to keep me from destructive behavior, and make me healthier. When I have not exercised for awhile or am overweight, start out gradually, so I will not sustain injuries. In multi-pet households, each cat should have its own time with you.

I get exercise by running, leaping, climbing, stalking, and pouncing. I will benefit from exercise in solitary play by clawing at my scratching post, leaping to the top of my cat tree or window perch. When you participate in my play by pulling a soft toy attached to an elastic cord, or by using any of the toys suggested on pages 80 and 81, I will receive robust exercise while you will benefit through laughter and amusement.

Cats find the outdoor environment exhilarating. After I have adjusted to my harness and leash, take me outdoors for a walk in good weather several times a week. I can also enjoy the out-of-doors by spending time on a screened porch or in an outdoor cat enclosure. (See PAWS to consider/SOME PURRfectly GOOD ADVICE, page 111.) Here I can observe the activities of birds and small mammals without becoming a menace. I can stalk them and even pounce within the confines of my secure enclosure. When you leave our home or before dark, remove me from my outdoor cat enclosure and bring me indoors.

Creating a stimulating environment for me requires that you provide a wide selection of safe toys. Toys inspire my natural curiosity, and curiosity is the key to feline intelligence. My level of intelligence will be directly related to the kind of environment I receive from YOU!

**TABBY TIP**
According to a survey by the American Pet Product Manufacturers, 3.1 toys are bought per year for a cat.

Many of the following toys can be made from items already on hand. The best feline toys meet the test of rollability, flopability, and crackleability!

1.  Hang a bird feeder outside my favorite window or place a <u>covered</u> fish aquarium in an area where I can observe the fish.
2.  Place cardboard tubes from toilet paper or paper towels on a hardwood floor. Any size cardboard cylinder will work as long as it is light enough for me to push. Provide large cardboard tubes for me to crawl through that are at least a foot in diameter. Tape the ends of a short tube, punch holes in the tube and place treats inside. When I roll the tube, a few treats will fall out giving more incentive to play.
3.  Place a pingpong ball on the floor, in the bathtub, or in an open tissue box for me to bat around. Then, enjoy my antics!
4.  Rub or spray catnip on my toys. (I may not be attracted to catnip until I am older.)
5.  Place cardboard boxes on the floor. Several boxes placed beside each other with entry from one box to the other is great fun.
6.  Take a paper grocery bag without handles and place it on its side on the floor for me to crawl into and explore. Never allow me to play in a plastic bag. (Although Dale has a dozen different toys, his favorite toy is a brown paper grocery bag tipped onto its side. Once inside the bag, his fierce kicking and rolling are heightened by the crackling sound of the paper. He spends about thirty seconds in the bag; then, tears through the house only to return to play in the bag again. After a day with Dale, the bag is reduced to tatters.)

7. Lay a sheet of crinkly paper on the floor; or make a loose wad of crinkly paper and toss it on the floor so I can pounce. I love things that crackle. Aluminum foil is not a good choice for this activity. If I swallow small pieces of the foil, they are not digestable and can cause an obstruction which may require surgery.

8. Place a small windup toy on the floor. If the toy does not make loud noises or otherwise scare me, I will follow it and pounce.

9. Play a video of birds, squirrels, and chipmunks. I will be captivated and try to follow the animals off the screen. I will look for openings where I can get into the television set, so make sure there are none.

10. Trail a small rope or feather behind you that is attached to a string to entice me to pounce. After playing with me, store this toy out of my reach. A mischievious kitten can become entangled in the string or rope.

11. Run a slow stream of cool water from a bathroom faucet. Cats enjoy sitting by the sink and batting at the water. However, make sure the toilet cover is down so I do not play in that water.

12. Buy me a furry mouse toy with a tail. I will enjoy tossing it in the air or grabbing the tail and swinging the "mouse" from side to side. If the mouse squeaks, all the better!

13. Provide rubber chew toys made for cats.

14. Mount a mirror where I can see myself or use a mirror or highly reflective object to project a light ray on a wall. Make sure I notice the spot of light and then slowly move it on the lower part of the wall where I can try to catch it. You can use a flashlight for the same purpose.

15. Provide climbing areas, window perches, and one or two scratching posts.

16. Read the newspaper while lying on the floor. This is a sure way to invite interaction.

17. Leave the radio or television on to keep me company while you are away.

18. Consider a second cat if your schedule does not allow time to play with me each day. Usually two cats will become companions.

19. Blow catnip bubbles. They are available at most pet stores and are as much fun for me as they are for you. If catnip is my thing, I will chase and paw the bubbles. They are non-toxic, but take care to keep the solution away from my eyes.

Watch to see which toys I enjoy the most. Rotate my favorites weekly. Squirrel the others away since my tastes may change. Replace worn, torn, or broken toys.

## I'M ONE DYNAMIC KITTY CAT

Adorable and cuddly, I'm a little ball of fluff
Exuding feline energy that lets me strut my stuff.

I'll race throughout the house as though a demon's on my trail
Performing flips and somersaults until I catch my tail.

I'm airborne in one flying leap to grab a ray or two
Of sunlight or a tiny speck invisible to you.

I'm geared to hunt and stalk my prey. I crouch. I leap and pounce
And quickly capture any toys that crackle, squeak, or bounce.

But soon my energetic play will show I'm highly skilled
For all around lay bushwhacked toys that I alone have 'killed.'

I'm one dynamic pussycat 'til someone shouts, "ENOUGH!
It's cat nap time for kitty cats who love to strut their stuff!"

PHOTOS OF ME AT PLAY

PHOTOS OF ME AT PLAY

# AWS to consider

SHOWTIME. Before considering showing me, you may want to visit a cat show as a spectator. This will acquaint you with the various procedures that occur at a show. Before entering a show, a purebred cat must be registered with Cat Fanciers' Association, Inc. (CFA). To request a registration form, write to: CFA, P.O. Box 1005, Manasquan, New Jersey 08736 or call 732-528-9797.

There are four major types of cat shows: Non-championship classes for kittens, and breeds not recognized by CFA; championship classes for registered cats of recognized breeds that have not been spayed or neutered; premiership classes for registered purebred cats that have been spayed or neutered; and household pets. The household pet classes are for cats of unknown lineage. *Cat Fancy* magazine usually has a list of upcoming shows. Contact the show's entry clerk at least eight weeks in advance in order to register. When registering, ask if there are helpful pamphlets for beginners. There is an entry and cage fee for each show. Fill out the registration paper carefully. Mistakes can disqualify me.

To enter the kitten class, I must be between four and eight months of age. I do not have to be neutered or spayed to be eligible. For the household pet category, I must be over eight months of age, spayed or neutered, but not declawed. I will be judged on my temperament, beauty, coloring, and grooming, and not by the written breed standard for registered purebred cats.

Championship classes are for cats eight months of age or older that are earning points toward the title of champion or grand champion. Premiership classes are for cats eight months of age or older that are earning points toward the title of premier or grand premier.

If you decide to show me, you will need the following items:

- a carrier and grooming supplies, including a claw trimmer
- a cover for the outside of the show cage and a soft mat for the inside
- clothespins to secure the outside covering
- non-scented disinfectant
- disposable litter boxes, litter and paper towels
- a food bowl, a water bowl and a supply of my food and treats
- bottles of our household water to avoid digestive problems
- a few favorite toys for comfort
- my health records and a first aid kit (See Some PURRfectly Good Advice/FIRST AID KITS, page 112).

Before going to a show, I must learn to accept a cage and get used to being handled. A cat that scratches the judge does not win points. When going to a show, I will need to have my claws clipped, my ears cleaned and be well groomed. All my vaccinations must be current, and I should be free of parasites and disease. Bring proof that I have been tested for feline leukemia and feline AIDS virus.

Take me to the cat show in my carrier which should be marked with your name, address and phone number. Arrive at a show early, so you will be relaxed. You do not want your tension transferred to me. At a show, cages are lined up or "benched" for competition. At registration, I will be given a "benching" number. This number will correspond with the number on the cage I will use at the show. Once you find my cage, it may be necessary to disinfect it before transferring me from my carrier. When I am inside the cage, partially cover it so I do not see other cats. If I am frightened by a neighboring cat, I may become too disturbed to be shown. Place my litter box and a few toys inside the cage. Give me food and water as needed. Listen for our number. When a judge announces my number, transfer me from the first cage to a cage by the judging area or "ring" that also has my benching number on it. You can stay with me until it is my turn to be judged. Then, I am on my own.

In the ring are long tables that the judges use. I will be removed from my cage and brought to one of the tables so a judge can examine me. If I am a registered purebred, I will be judged by a standard for my breed. After I am examined, the judge will place any ribbons I have earned on my cage.

You may want to attend a cat show even if you choose not to show me. As well as having fun, you will pick up pointers on cat care and my particular breed.

My Cat Fanciers' Association registration number is _____

My first show was on _____ at _____

I was entered in the _____ class.

When the judge handled me, I responded by _____

_____

The judge said, " _____ "

I received a _____

I need to improve my _____

My owner needs to improve _____

## CAT TYPES?

Bobcat, cool cat, fat cat, alley cat,
Tomcat, pole cat, wild cat, pussy cat,
Snowcat, copy cat, LOVE A CAT!

# PHOTOS OF MY FIRST SHOW <u>OR</u> JUST SHOWING OFF

# WAYS I SHOW OFF MY KITTY STUFF

_____

_____

_____

_____

_____

_____

_____

_____

_____

_____

_____

_____

_____

_____

_____

_____

_____

_____

# PAWS to consider

**SPAYING AND NEUTERING.** I would like to present you with a math problem. If I am bred and all of my offspring are allowed to breed, how many kitties would be living in our home in seven years. According to the Humane Society of the United States, the answer is **theoretically 420,000!** That should be reason enough to spay or neuter me!

Even if you think I am the most adorable, smartest, and finest cat in the world, and you promise to find marvelous homes for all my offspring, breeding me cannot be justified. There are millions of adorable, smart, and fine cats in the world that need marvelous homes.  Volunteer at your local shelter and you will quickly understand why there is no need to bring more cats into the world at this time. Finding homes for all my kittens will eliminate homes that would be available for kittens from no-kill shelters.

Spaying a female cat means you will not have to worry about attempts to escape and roam, howling, spraying, or personality changes when in heat. Neutering a male cat will eliminate unpleasant tomcat traits, such as aggression; marking the inside of our home with urine; or caterwauling when it is time to mate. Spaying or neutering increases my life expectancy by two to three years. It reduces the risk of breast cancer, uterine infections, prostate problems, and testicular tumors. It also produces a more even disposition in most cats. It does not make a cat prone to obesity — only overfeeding can accomplish that.

A female cat should be spayed before her first estrous or "heat" period (around four to six months of age). In North America, the heat season is usually between mid-January and late September, but can vary, depending on exposure to tomcats, warm climates and other cycling females. A cat can cycle every two weeks. A male cat should be neutered after becoming sexually mature, usually between four to six months. The timing for neutering and spaying may vary according to breed. The cost of the operations is reasonable and much cheaper than caring for a litter of kittens. However, if it is too costly for you, contact Spay/USA (800-248-7729) for low-cost spay/neuter services in your area.

The authors invite you to be part of the solution to the overpopulation of cats in the United States. Eight to ten million dogs and cats are taken to animal shelters every year. Four to five million are euthanized each year because there are not enough homes for them. In <u>Puppy Stuff</u>, the authors included a section on breeding. Since that time they have seen firsthand the hardships that result from excessive breeding and have decided not to include that section in <u>Kitty Stuff</u>. Breeding me can stress your energy and your pocketbook, and has no bearing on the quality of my life. If you feel your children must see the birth process to appreciate the miracle of life, buy a picture book or rent a video showing kittens being born. If you feel I need a feline companion or you want more cats, please consider adopting or buying one of the countless homeless kittens or cats in shelters across the country?

I was spayed/neutered (date) _____

# SIX TO NINE MONTHS

I weigh _____ at six months, _____ at seven months, _____ at eight months

and _____ at nine months.

I am _____ inches tall at six months, _____ inches tall at seven months, _____

inches tall at eight months and _____ inches tall at nine months.

I shredded _____

I am now a "teenager" and was dumbfounded by my "parent's" reaction (Yes/No) or _____

_____

I sometimes stare at _____

I spontaneously _____

When transported in a pet carrier, I never make a fuss _____, growl _____,

never keep quiet _____, or _____

Besides going to the veterinarian, I like to ride to _____

_____ with _____ because _____

_____

I took my first trip to _____

I went by car _____, airplane _____, or _____

I was a _____ traveler.

I am not fond of travel. My "parent(s)" left me with _____

My "parent(s)" traveled to _____

My "parent(s)" bought me a _____

My caregiver reported that I _____

_____

 **AWS to consider**

TRAVEL. Cats are not particularly fond of travel. In fact, for some, it is equal to coughing up a hairball. I should _not_ travel when I am ill; a female in heat; or younger than the age of twelve weeks. Before traveling with me, take time to prepare me for the trip.

First, let's consider car travel. While in a car, I must always be in a carrier that is secured by  one of the seatbelts. The carrier should be large enough for me to stand and turn around. It prevents me from jumping onto your lap or getting under your feet while you are driving and from being injured if you stop suddenly. Before taking me in a car, allow me to become acquainted with my carrier. (See PAWS to consider/TRAINING, page 63.) Some cats are  never comfortable in a carrier or in a car. They are much happier at home with a pet sitter when you travel.

If I have adjusted to the carrier, introduce me gradually to car travel by taking short trips. Most cats do not suffer from motion sickness. They are protected by an anatomical structure in the inner ear which also contributes to their superb balance. If I am the exception, my veterinarian can prescribe medication for motion sickness or tranquilizers. However, there are risks with tranquilizers which should be discussed with my veterinarian. It is best to leave me at home in the care of a pet sitter if I am a queasy or nervous traveler.

When we are traveling by car, exercise me each morning before departing. Stop often during the trip to allow me fresh water, exercise, and elimination. Place my litter box on the floor of the car and adjust the windows so I cannot escape. Let me out of my carrier. Give me time to stretch, walk around the car and use the litter box. If I have adjusted to a harness and leash, take me for a short walk. Watch for hazards, such as the sudden presence of an unrestrained dog. Be prepared to pick me up immediately. Never leave me in a car in extreme weather because heat stroke or hypothermia can be life threatening. If you must leave me for a short time during warm weather, roll the windows down a few inches and please hurry back. A cat is a prime target for theft when left alone in a car with slightly open windows. Better yet, place me in my carrier and take me with you. At the end of each day's travel, give me food, water, and exercise.

When making travel plans, be sure the facility where you will be staying allows pets. The AAA Pet Book lists over ten thousand pet friendly, AAA rated accommodations. In addition, it offers practical advice about traveling with your pet. Petswelcome.com maintains more than 25,000 listings of pet-friendly travel accommodations. In addition, their service offers air travel, emergency veterinarians, pet sitters, and kennel information. If you cannot find accommodations that accept pets, ask about a reputable kennel in your travel area. When I am with you in a motel/hotel, be a considerate guest. Do not let me soil the carpet or destroy property. We want the facility to continue to welcome other pet owners. Check out the room for any hiding places or hazards before releasing me from my carrier. When you leave the room, place me in my carrier. Place the "Do Not Disturb" sign on the door so no one will enter while you are away. If the room has recently been sprayed with insecticide, ask for another room. The spray is not healthy for me.

Before traveling, all of my inoculations should be up to date. Bring my health certificate showing my inoculations and general health status. This is important in case I require medical attention, kennel boarding, or entrance to another country. Consult my veterinarian to see if the area to which I am traveling is an area where heartworm is prevalent. If I am not taking the heartworm preventative, start it four weeks before leaving. Ask my veterinarian how long I should continue the preventative after we return home.

When traveling with me, consider packing the following:

- health certificate
- grooming equipment including a claw trimmer
- food and water bowl, a supply of cat food and cat treats
  (It is best not to change my diet. Water can be changed gradually over the course of the trip.)
- a few favorite toys
- plastic bags and a scoop or paper towels for clean up

- a well-ventilated carrier with a secure latch
- prescribed medications and motion sickness medicine, if needed
- a disposable or regular litter box and litter
- a leash and H-type harness with identification tags
- a photo of me in case I become lost
- flea and tick medication
- a first aid kit (See PAWS to consider/Some PURRfectly Good Advice, page 112)

When traveling other than by car, check with the carrier about its requirements for transporting animals. If traveling by air, I can stay in the cabin, provided that I am confined in a Sherpa bag or cat carrier that fits under the seat. Generally, the dimension of the carrier cannot be larger than twenty-one inches long by thirteen inches wide by nine inches high. Check with our carrier for exact measurements. A health certificate is required by airlines. The certificate is valid for ten days from the date of issuance. A reservation is needed due to a limited number of animals allowed on each flight. When you are passing through security you will be required to remove me from my carrier. Therefore, it is best if I am wearing a harness and leash with an identification tag. When removing me from my carrier, reach in and firmly grip the leash and the back of the harness with one hand. Gently pull me out of the carrier and support my weight with your other hand and arm. This should keep me from escaping if I become frightened. (While Jodi was on vacation, Miss Flori adopted her. When Jodi tried to bring Miss Flori back to Illinois, they experienced airline problems two days in a row. Jodi and Miss Flori passed through security three times and Jodi quickly learned the value of a leash and harness or there might have been one very frightened cat running around the Orlando, Florida airport.)

If we plan to travel outside the continental United States, communicate well in advance with the state or with the consulate of the country of destination for regulations regarding entry. Hawaii, for example, has a quarantine period before I can be allowed to join you. The consulate of a country will generally be located in Washington, D.C.

Although airlines have developed more humane policies toward crated pets traveling in cargo holds, my authors do not recommend transporting a cat in the cargo section of an airline unless there is no alternative. If it is absolutely necessary to use cargo, place me in my carrier or one that you rent from the airline. The carrier should be large enough for me to stand, turn around, and lie on my side. It must be sturdy, easy to open, and without sharp protrusions. It must be <u>well</u> ventilated, and have 3"-4" rims that prevent shifting cargo from blocking my air supply. Mark the carrier "This End UP" with directional arrows and label "Live Animal" or "Animals" in letters at least one inch high on the top and two sides. The carrier must have handles so airline personnel can easily lift it. For long flights, food and water dishes should be secured to the inside of my carrier. My food should be sealed inside a plastic bag. The bag and my feeding schedule should be attached to the <u>outside</u> of my carrier. Line my carrier with absorbent bedding. The airline will require my health certificate issued within ten days of the trip, a plane ticket, and identification tags both on my carrier and my break-away collar. The identification tags should include your name, home address, and phone number, destination address and phone number, and my name. Feed me a light meal well in advance of the trip and exercise me shortly before departure. Withhold water one hour prior to departure unless the weather is hot. Empty the water dish before departure.

Air travel is hard on cats. I should not be shipped by air before the age of three months. Travel is not recommended for cats that are ill, elderly, very young, or pregnant. A pug-nosed cat, such as a Persian, may have difficulty breathing during air travel. Tranquilizers are not recommended because the effects at high altitudes are uncertain.

It is your responsibility to monitor my travel. The greatest danger to me is extreme temperature both inside and outside the aircraft. The plane's cargo section is not cooled or heated. Choose morning or evening flights during summer months when the weather will be cooler. When possible, my flight should be non-stop. Ask if pets are last on and first off the cargo section. For travel that includes a plane change, inquire with the airlines about where my carrier will be placed while I wait. Six hours is considered the maximum time I should be kept in my crate. For confinement longer than six hours, consider another means of transportation. Talk with my veterinarian before planning air travel.

"On Board With Your Pet" or "Car Travel With Your Pet" can be obtained from The American Society for the Prevention of Cruelty to Animals by sending a self-addressed, stamped envelope to: ASPCA, attention: Public Information Dept., 424 E. 92nd St., New York, NY 10128. For additional information about pet travel, visit the Humane Society of the United States' web site at www.hsus.org.

The following are telephone numbers for some of the airlines that transport pets:

- American Airlines, Priority Parcel, 800-227-4622
- Continental Airlines, Quickpac, 800-575-3335
- Delta Airlines, Delta Dash, 800-221-1212 (for carry-on pet reservations) or 888-736-3738 (for cargo reservations)
- Northwest Airlines, Priority Pet Center, 888-692-4738
- US Air, 800-428-4322

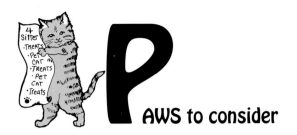

# PAWS to consider

**PET SITTERS/BOARDING KENNELS.** You may find it difficult the first time you have to leave me in the care of someone else. However, knowing that you have chosen a qualified pet sitter or a clean and safe kennel facility should bring you peace of mind. A reputable boarding kennel should not accept me until I have had the full benefit of my inoculations. Before visiting with pet sitters or kennels, obtain recommendations from friends or my veterinarian.

Cats are sensitive to change. Because I may fare better in my own familiar surroundings, I adjust well when a pet sitter is hired to feed, exercise, and care for me at home during your absence. My authors recommend the use of a reputable pet sitter when a responsible friend or family member is unavailable to care for me while you are away. Some pet sitters even bring in the mail, water houseplants, and rotate the lights. Make sure the pet sitter is licensed, insured, bonded, trained in animal first aid and CPR, and provides references. Using a pet sitter once before you leave will let you observe how the sitter treats me; it will give me time to become familiar with the sitter. Do not expect us to become buddies in just one short visit. Cats need time to adjust to new people and new situations.

A mouse was in charge of a cat,
That needed to be babysat.
The story is weird.
How the mouse disappeared.
And the truth is known
Just to the cat!

When leaving me in the care of a pet sitter, confine me to a safe room where I cannot be destructive. The sitter can more easily find me and attend to my needs, knowing I am in a specific room. Do not confine me to my crate which will not allow me adequate exercise. Leave some of my toys, my litter box, scratching post, and food and water bowls in my room. Do not place the litter box near the food and water bowls. Leave instructions for the sitter in a previously agreed-upon location. (See **CAT SITTER CARDS** at the back of book). Notify the sitter when you arrive home or if you will be detained. For information about hiring a pet sitter, call the National Association of Professional Pet Sitters (717-691-5565) or visit their web site at www.petsitters.org., or call Pet Sitters International (336-983-9222) or visit their web site at www.petsit.com.

If you decide to board me at a kennel, make a surprise visit to kennels in your area and ask for a tour. During the tour, check water, food bowls and litter boxes to make sure they are clean. If you are denied a tour, look for another kennel. Most kennels have large cat cages. Some luxury kennels offer an actual room and bed. Some veterinarians have boarding facilities, which may be a good option if I am taking medication.

When considering a kennel, the following are some guidelines to consider:

- What is the kennel's philosophy about cat care? Does it agree with your own?
- Are the premises clean? Is there a disagreeable odor permeating the facility?

- Are the cat cages in good condition? Is the cage large enough for me to move around. Is there an adjoining cage or adequate room for my litter box?
- Before accepting me, does the kennel require proof that I have been tested for leukemia and feline AIDS virus and have all my inoculations?
- Are the staff gentle when handling me?
- Does the kennel have a first aid kit? Are the staff knowledgeable enough to know if I need medical attention? Will they accept me if I am taking medication?
- Is the kennel bonded and insured?
- Is the kennel heated and air-conditioned? Is there an alarm if the temperature rises or falls to a dangerous level?
- Is the kennel secure? Does it have a fire alarm? Is my area safe from dogs? (Dogs should be housed in a separate area so they do not stress the cats.)
- Do the staff fill out forms concerning my needs, such as exercise, food, medications, and veterinarian name? Do they allow you to bring my food from home?
- Is someone on duty at all times? If not, what arrangements are made for my safety?

For a list of recommended kennels, call the American Boarding Kennels Association (719-667-1600). Visit their web site at www.abka.com for more information on boarding pets.

Once you have chosen a boarding kennel, take the following with you when I will be boarded:

- proof and dates of my inoculations
- medications, if needed, with clear instructions for use
- complete food supply and treats; I may have problems adjusting to a new diet
- a few favorite toys and something of yours, like an old sock, that carries your scent to make me feel secure
- two rugs for sleeping. If one is soiled, a clean one can be put down. Make sure I cannot pull pieces off the rug that, if ingested, could choke me
- veterinarian's name and phone number; and a number where you, a friend, or relative can be reached; and any needed instructions (See **CAT KENNEL CARDS** at back of book.)

We kitties sometimes suffer from separation anxiety when we are away from our "parent(s)". To keep my feelings of separation from becoming severe, leave me at the kennel for a few hours or for day care once or twice before you take a trip. When I learn that you will return, I will be better able to adjust. This reduces the likelihood of serious problems when you are away for a longer time. Before leaving me, check with the kennel about its pet pick-up schedule.

When leaving me with a friend or relative, ask that I be kept in an area free from poisonous plants or other cat hazards. (See PAWS to consider/SAFETY, page 32.) If the caregiver owns a dog, ask that I be kept in a dog-free area. Take my food, litter box, bedding, and some toys. It is not wise to change any of these items. I will feel more secure with my own things. Changing my diet can upset my tummy. The caregiver should have my carrier in case I need to go to my veterinarian. Leave instructions for my care. (See **CAT SITTER CARDS** at the back of the book.) Before you depart, let me visit the caregiver's home to familiarize myself with the new surroundings.

PHOTOS OF ME ON MY FIRST TRIP
OR ME WITH MY FAVORITE PET SITTER

# PAWS to consider

**LOST KITTIES.** I know that you take exceptionally good care of me; however, out of curiosity, I may dart out a door that was accidentally left open. Once outdoors, I may panic and run away. Without identification it may be impossible to reunite us. There are four forms of identification available: microchips, ID tags, tattoos, and ear tags. It is important to use one of them.

**TABBY TIP**
According to the American Humane Association, only 2% of cats entering shelters are returned to their owners.

**MICROCHIP.** A microchip, which is about the size of a piece of long grain rice, is encoded with a series of numbers and injected under the skin between my shoulders by my veterinarian. The microchip is encased in a biocompatible non-reactive capsule that does not irritate pets. The process is safe and relatively painless. In fact, it can be done while I am awake. Two companies that market microchips are Avid, producing "Friendchip" and Schering-Plough Animal Health Corp. producing "HomeAgain". Universal scanners, which detect signals from either chip, are made available to shelters by both companies. "HomeAgain" has a pet registry with the American Kennel Club and Avid has its own registry, Pettrac. Both registry facilities are open twenty-four hours a day and both require a one-time registration fee. Update your information in the database if your address or phone number changes. For more information, call "Friendchip", 800-336-2843, or "HomeAgain", 800-341-5785.

**ID TAG.** A breakaway collar with a tag can be used. The tag should bear your name, address, phone number, and my name. Check the tag occasionally to make sure the information is still legible. If you use an ID tag, I should <u>always</u> wear my collar and tag. If I can easily dislodge my collar, consider another form of identification. Should I become lost outdoors, I could snag the collar on a low branch and pull the collar off. The authors strongly suggest two forms of identification when one of the forms is a breakaway collar and tag.

**TATTOO.** A tattoo is permanent and visible. The tattoo is applied to the inside of my ear where my hair will not obscure the markings. Tattoo numbers can also be printed on the tag attached to my collar. The tattoo must be registered. For information and registration, call 800-828-8667 or visit www.tattoo-a-pet.com. A tattoo should not be applied before I am six months old.

**EAR TAG.** The Ear Tag® is made of surgical quality stainless steel and is removable for cleaning. The tag is octagonal and an eighth of an inch in diameter. It is placed at the base of my ear and does not interfere with my ear rotation. My veterinarian should install the tag. The procedure is relatively painless. Our phone number or my veterinarian's phone number, plus a personal ID number, can be imprinted on the tag. An ear tag should not be used on me until my ears are fully developed, which is between four and five months of age.

The following are tips to minimize the chances of my becoming lost or stolen:

- Train me to stay indoors. (See PAWS to consider/TRAINING, page 62.)
- Neuter or spay me so I will not have a desire to dart out the door and roam.
- Secure me during potentially frightening times, such as fireworks displays or thunderstorms.
- Secure car windows and door locks when traveling with me. Better yet, take me with you in my carrier whenever possible.
- Secure me in one room with a "Do Not Enter" sign when packing to move to another location.

If I should become lost or stolen, you may find it necessary to do one or more of the following:

- As soon as you notice that I am missing, drive and walk through our neighborhood calling my name and asking people if they have seen me.
- Check places near the house where I might be trapped or hiding.
- Place my litter box, something of yours, and one of my favorite toys outdoors. My sense of smell is very keen and the scent from one of these items may lead me home.
- Place posters with my picture and description within a sixty-mile radius of my home. It is amazing how far and fast a frightened cat can travel. On the poster, list the date lost. Include your phone number and the fact that you are offering a reward. Give a poster to delivery people that frequent the neighborhood. Ask them to tell you if they see me or, better yet, bring me home. Place a poster in nearby stores.
- Enlist neighborhood children's help because children are outdoors more than adults. Tell them about a reward.
- Contact veterinary clinics, boarding kennels, humane societies, and animal shelters, give each a clear description and, if possible, a photo of me. Keep in touch every few days. Tell them which form of identification I use.
- Place a newspaper or radio ad. Offer a reward.
- Contact laboratory facilities at local universities and hospitals to make sure that I have not been sold to them. Send a flyer with my photo to these facilities.
- Contact the highway department to inquire if an injured cat has been found. If so, check to see if it is me.
- Call Pet Club of America at (800) 666-5678. This is a nonprofit lost and found service that has been recovering missing pets since 1976.
- Call the police department if you think I have been stolen.
- If I am lost while you are traveling, and you must move on, leave your name and phone number, my picture and description, and my form of identification with the motel/hotel management and the local animal shelter.

After offering a reward, someone may call claiming to have found me. Meet the person in a public area. Do not give the reward until I am safely returned.

## NINE TO TWELVE MONTHS

I weigh _____ at nine months, _____ at ten months, _____ at eleven months and _____ at twelve months.

I am _____ tall at nine months, _____ at ten months, _____ at eleven months and _____ at twelve months.

I love creature comforts. My favorite places to luxuriate are _____

_____

I like to lie on clothes fresh from the dryer. Yes/No (circle one) or I like to lie on _____

_____

I like to ambush _____

I like to look out the window at _____

I like to lie on top of the _____

and look down at _____

I like to watch the following on television: _____

When small animals or birds appear on television, I _____

_____

My favorite treat is _____

My favorite pet playmate's name is _____

My "parent(s)" has successfully trained me to _____

_____

_____

I still get the upper paw by _____

My most adorable trait is _____

My _____ is my most beautiful feature.

## THE KITTY RAP

I am a people kitty. I'm the envy of all cats.
For in my people family, a cat wears many hats!

I'm pet, companion, confidant, and minder of the store,
An automatic wake-up call; chief greeter at the door!

Sometimes the grown-ups in my house will tend to oversleep.
My job of gentle prodding is to make them sit and speak!

A nudge, a lick, a well-placed paw, is all it ever takes,
To make them holler, "Yikes", "Good grief!"
And "Oh, For heaven's sake!"

So when I get them up and going, then my life is sweet,
That's when I get my breakfast and they all come down
to eat!

I'm basking on a sunny sill as kids tramp off to
school.
'Cause taking time for naps should be a feline's
foremost rule!

But naps must end although the time was put to
such good use.
Then, BOOM! The kids are home again and
everything breaks loose!

We run and play at hide-and-seek right up 'til dinner time,
Tonight each person said to me, "I'm happy you are mine!"

# PHOTOS WITH MY BEST ANIMAL AND HUMAN FRIENDS

# PURRsonals
## A STORY OR POEM ABOUT MY HUMAN AND ME DOIN' FUN THINGS

_____

_____

_____

_____

_____

_____

_____

_____

_____

_____

_____

_____

_____

_____

_____

_____

_____

# PAWS to consider

ONE YEAR AND BEYOND. I am now a young adult cat. Your training, consistency, patience, love, and good care have helped me become a well-behaved friend who will be loyal to you for the rest of my life.  At one year of age, I can be weaned to a <u>nutritionally complete</u> adult cat food that can be used for the next seven years. Change my food gradually, mixing the new food with the old. Observe my stool for problems. If necessary, consult my veterinarian.  When you use dry food, consider self-feeding.  This method involves filling my bowl daily with the correct amount of food for my size and leaving the food down all the time. When using canned food, I can be fed twice a day in portions correct for my size. Several cat foods and treats are available to help control the formation of hairballs. In addition to my food, add a few appropriate cat treats between meals; especially treats that help prevent tarter build-up on my teeth. I <u>must</u> have fresh cool water available at all times in at least two locations.  Male cats in particular are prone to bladder disease, so good hydration is important. If I am in good health, I will require a veterinary visit once a year for a physical exam and booster shots. You may want to consider a pet insurance plan. As with human health insurance, cost depends on my age and pre-existing conditions. Insurance can cover everything from routine vaccination to surgery.

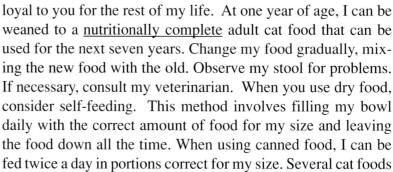

## TABBY TIPS

Use foods tested by the Association of American Feed Control Officials (look for endorsement on package.)

At eight to ten years of age, I will start to enter my "golden years".  The average cat lives fifteen years, but some have been known to live to the age of twenty-four. As I start to age, my metabolism changes, I will need fewer calories and less protein. Use a nutritionally complete senior or geriatric food for the remainder of my life. Ask my veterinarian for advice about various foods available.

Older cats are more prone to disease, especially, hyperthyroidism, chronic renal failure, hypertension, cancer, diabetes mellitus, and inflammatory bowel disease. With your veterinarian's help, become familiar with the symptoms of these diseases. Early detection is important. After my eighth birthday, take me to the veterinarian twice a year. At this age, a complete blood count and blood chemistry profile is a good idea. Blood tests can detect disease before symptoms are apparent or establish a baseline if I am healthy. If I exhibit symptoms, such as vomiting, frequent diarrhea, a failure to eat or drink, increased appetite and water intake, a persistent cough, rapid breathing, hyperactivity, lethargy, or weight loss take me to my veterinarian.  These symptoms could signal a serious illness.

Tooth loss and gum disease are more prevalent as I grow older and may cause eating problems. Dental check-ups are essential and, if needed, professional dental cleaning. Poor dental health can cause bacteria to enter my bloodstream through inflamed bleeding gums and cause heart, liver, or kidney problems.  (See PAWS to consider/DENTAL HYGIENE, page 51, for symptoms of periodontal disease.)

As I grow older, I may lose my hearing, suffer impaired vision, increase my sleep periods or develop arthritis. If I develop arthritis, make my life easier by providing a comfortable

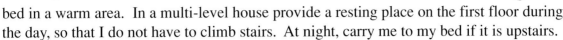

bed in a warm area. In a multi-level house provide a resting place on the first floor during the day, so that I do not have to climb stairs. At night, carry me to my bed if it is upstairs.

Sometimes I may be cranky if awakened from a nap or startled. My crankiness may be from the pain of arthritis. Placing my food and water dishes in an elevated stand may ease my pain if I have developed arthritis in my neck. Do not place my food and water bowls in areas that require high leaps. Sometimes, as an older cat, I may have accidents. Do not scold or punish me. Ask my veterinarian to examine me for bladder or bowel problems. If accidents are due to old age or arthritis, place my litter box near my bed and one or two litter boxes in other areas that I use. Buy a litter box with lower sides if I have difficulty climbing into the box. If my sight is impaired, do not change the location of my litter box, or food and water dishes. Sight impaired cats rely on their excellent senses of smell, hearing, and touch. Put yourself in my paws and be patient.

Geriatric cats sharpen their claws less frequently, so you may need to trim my claws more often. Brush me regularly because I may not be as agile as I once was or as meticulous about my grooming. While brushing me, check my body for tumors. Older cats are prone to develop them. If a tumor is found, take me to my veterinarian to make sure it is benign. Continue to monitor the tumor for change. If change occurs, check with my veterinarian. If I suddenly pull away during grooming, it may indicate that my skin is sensitive. Use a brush made for sensitive skin or a comb for my grooming. Continue to exercise me through play, but as I age, make the action gentler and slower. Because I cannot move or scratch myself as easily as I used to, keep me indoors where insects cannot bite me.

Try not to change my routine since I may be set in my ways and a little stubborn. If you are going to travel and have not placed me in a kennel before, do not start now. Use a pet sitter. I could be greatly stressed by the separation from you and my home, and become ill.

As I grow older treat me with respect and love and I will respond accordingly.

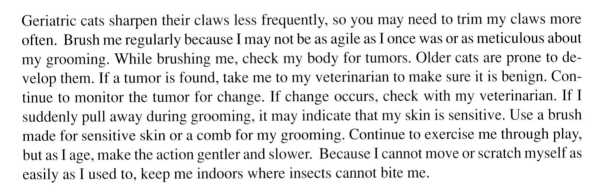

## CAT YEARS
(My age in human years. This is an average.)

| CAT | | HUMAN | CAT | | HUMAN |
|---|---|---|---|---|---|
| 1 year | = | 16 | 11 years | = | 58 |
| 2 years | = | 21 | 12 years | = | 62 |
| 3 years | = | 26 | 13 years | = | 66 |
| 4 years | = | 30 | 14 years | = | 70 |
| 5 years | = | 34 | 15 years | = | 74 |
| 6 years | = | 38 | 16 years | = | 78 |
| 7 years | = | 42 | 17 years | = | 82 |
| 8 years | = | 46 | 18 years | = | 86 |
| 9 years | = | 50 | 19 years | = | 90 |
| 10 years | = | 54 | 20 years | = | 94 |

ONE YEAR

I weigh _____.

1 am _____ tall.

Now that I am all grown up, my "parent(s)" describes my

temperament as calm _____ , hyperactive _____ ,

easily excited _____ , aggressive _____ , aloof _____ ,

friendly _____ , lazy _____ , or _____

_____

I celebrated my birthday with _____

I had a special treat of _____

For my birthday, I received _____

_____

On my "parent's" birthday I gave him/her a _____

MY BIRTHDAY PHOTO

# PURRsonals

## SPECIAL OCCASIONS

On my first Christmas or Hanukkah I was _____ old.

I received _____

I ate _____

I liked _____

I was attracted to the Christmas tree or Minorah because _____

_____

I _____ the Christmas tree, _____

the presents and _____ the ornaments.

# MY CHRISTMAS OR HANUKKAH PICTURES

# A DAY IN MY LIFE

My life is simply just a lark,
I eat and **sleep** and play till dark,
Provoke the dog to hear it bark,
And leave my scent to make my mark.
**This hectic life I lead calls for a snooze!**

My people play with me each day,
And make requests like "come" and "stay,"
They give me lots of praise and say,
It's such a treat when I obey.
**Just lead me to my bed. I need a rest!**

The tot is someone I adore
For he drops crumbs upon the floor.
I track him down for treats galore;
My friend, the little cookie store.
**He wore me out. I must catch 40 winks!**

The little girl and I have tea.
Her doll joins in and that makes three.
And when we chat, we all agree...
I've had enough. I must be free!
**Society affairs require a nap!**

The kids and I are stuck like glue,
And pass the time in fun, we do.
They pull a toy that I pursue,
And then there's something else to do.
**My shades are going down. I'm fast asleep!**

I'll see my clinic vets at three,
And take a color print of me
To put in their menagerie
Of snapshots of the pets they see.
**A yawn is comin' on. I'll hit the hay!**

There's just one scene I can't ignore,
A dog asleep upon the floor,
With twitching paws and rhythmic snore,
I yowl, I pounce...
**Oh, what the heck! I think I'll take a snooze!**

# A TYPICAL DAY IN MY LIFE

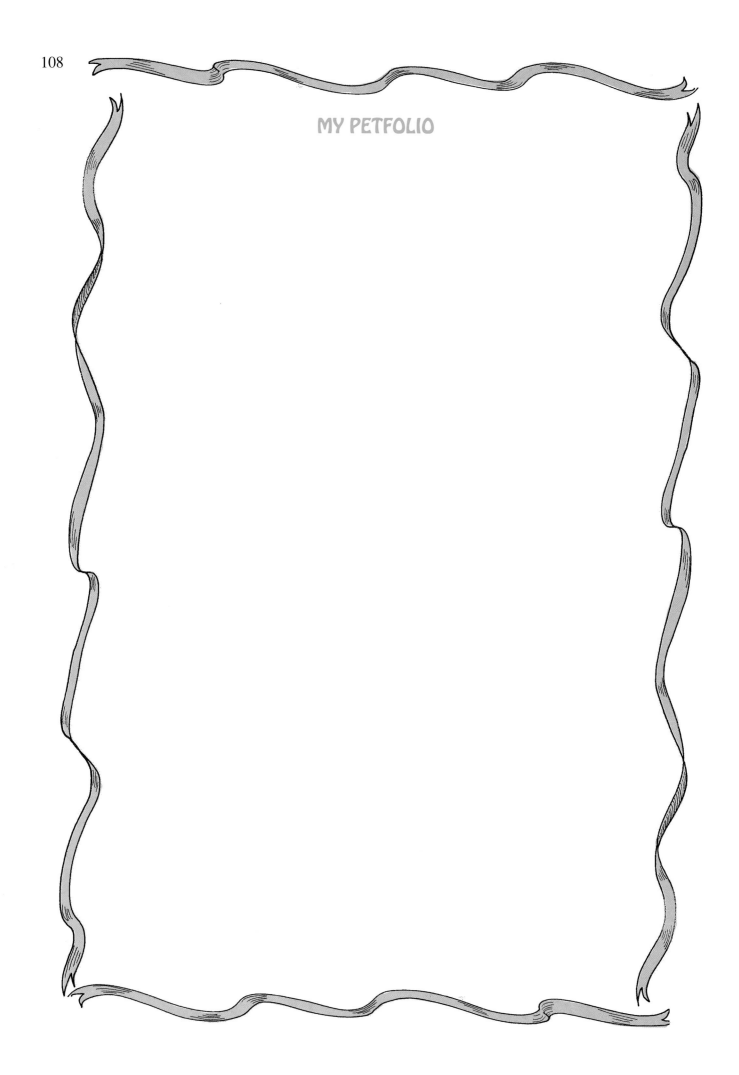

MY PETFOLIO

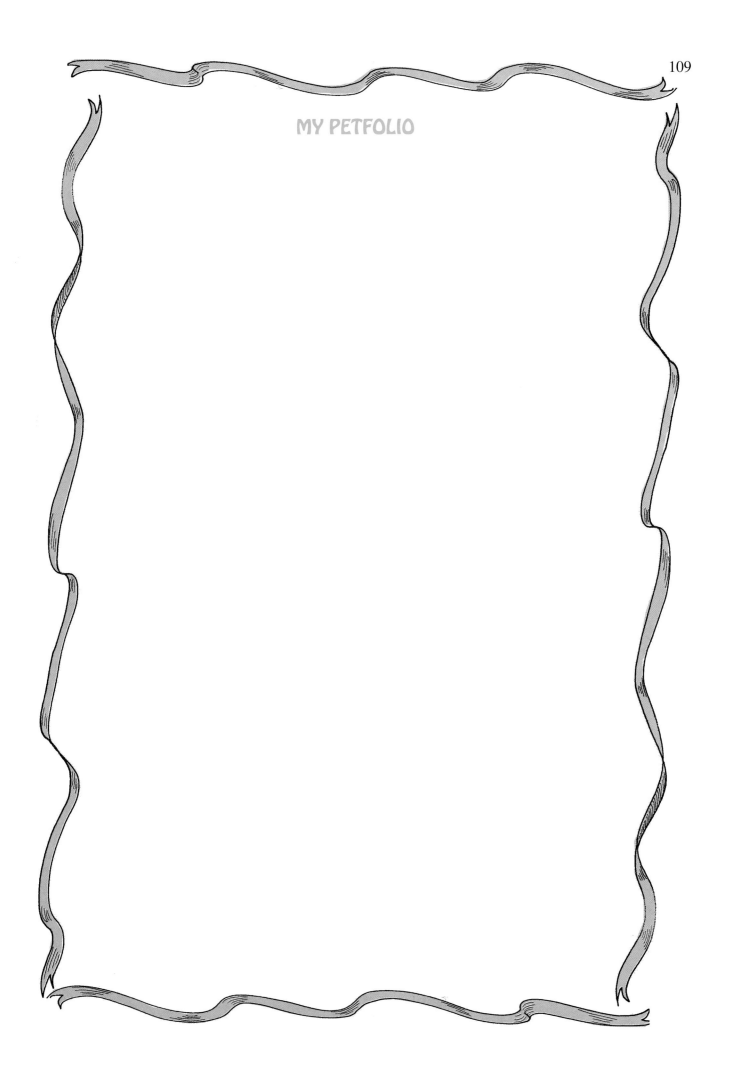

MY PETFOLIO

# Some PURRfectly Good Advice

**ADMINISTERING MEDICINES.** Medication should be given only on the advice of my veterinarian. The easiest way to give me a pill is to put the pill inside a bite-sized ball of flavorful food. Check with my veterinarian to determine which foods are compatible with the medication I am taking. Some hard pills can be crushed and sprinkled on canned food. If I will not take my medicine in my food, ask my veterinarian to show you how to properly give me a pill or try the following: place your left hand on top of my head with your thumb and forefinger at the corners of my mouth. Tip my head back until my nose points straight up and my mouth opens. Do not attempt to open my mouth by pulling down on my lower jaw. You will be unable to open my mouth properly and may injure me. Once my mouth is open, hold the pill between the thumb and forefinger of your right hand, and place the pill as far back on my tongue as possible. Close my mouth and hold it gently. With your right hand, rub the front of my neck to stimulate swallowing. Practice this procedure a few times by placing a piece of tasty food in my mouth. Practicing with food makes it easier to give me a pill later. If you are unsuccessful with these methods, purchase a pill gun. My veterinarian will demonstrate how to use it.

To give medicine in liquid form, wrap me in a towel and place me in an upright position. Using a nonbreakable liquid medicine dispenser, fill the dispenser with the proper amount of medication. Pull outward on the loose skin on the <u>side</u> of my bottom jaw. This will act as a funnel. Release the medication slowly into my mouth. Quickly, but gently, place your hand around my muzzle to keep my mouth closed. Tilt my head slightly upward while stroking my neck with your other hand until I swallow the medication. If I start to choke or cough, lower my head immediately. Dispensing liquid medicine too rapidly or into the front of my mouth can cause aspiration pneumonia.

**ALLERGIES.** Signs of allergies in cats are itchy skin and sneezing. The most common types of allergies are flea and atopy (inhalant allergy). Less common are food or contact allergies.

A flea allergy can cause hair loss and skin lesions that must be treated. The ongoing process of controlling fleas in my area is very important. (See PAWS to consider/EXTERNAL PARASITES, page 56.) Contact my veterinarian if you suspect a flea allergy. Medicine may be prescribed to stop the itch/scratch cycle.

Atopic allergies may cause me to lick my feet; rub my face on the floor or furniture; sneeze or excessively scratch my body. My veterinarian can test for atopic allergies by taking a blood sample and checking it for antibodies to different allergens, or by intradermal skin testing. I must be sedated for the skin test. Some hair is removed and I am injected with tiny doses of antigens. My skin is then monitored for a reaction to the antigens. Once allergens are identified, I can be desensitized by receiving allergy antigen injections. Shots take six to twelve months to be effective. If possible, avoid the allergens.

**TABBY TIPS**
A cat is subject to the same problem as a human when it inhales secondhand cigarette smoke.

Food allergies usually cause itching in the area of my head or ears. If a food allergy is suspected, feed me food containing a new protein source such as ham, duck, rabbit, or venison. Gradually replace the food I am eating with the new food. Feed me only the new food for six weeks. If I improve, continue the new food and gradually introduce treats one at a time. If I show no improvement, try the same method using another protein source or ask my veterinarian to test for food allergies.

Contact allergies are rare for cats. However, I can develop an allergy to my flea collar. Symptoms are redness and irritation of the skin. Removing the allergens and treating the skin with a topical ointment prescribed by a veterinarian usually solves the problem.

Sometimes a cat's "parent(s)" can become allergic to their cat. It is the dander, which are tiny particles of loose skin, or a cat's saliva that causes the allergy. Controlling dander helps control the allergy. For more information about allergies visit the website www.petallergy.com.

The following suggestions may be helpful in reducing an allergic reaction:

- Wash your hands after handling me.
- Do not allow me to sleep in your bedroom.
- Wipe my hair daily or weekly with a commercial anti-allergy pet solution depending on the severity of the allergy.
- Choose someone else to groom me.
- Consider the purchase of a HEPA air filter unit and vacuum frequently.

CAT ENCLOSURE KITS. C & D Pet Products, Inc. makes a cat enclosure kit that is approved by the American Society for the Prevention of Cruelty to Animals. The enclosure is made of solid redwood and 2" x 3" galvanized wire. The kit has three sides, a top, a door and three shelves. It is approximately 6' x 6' x 6'. It can be purchased by calling 888-554-7387 or visiting their web site at www.cdpets.com. Kitten wire is available.

DISASTER PREPAREDNESS. Have a plan for my rescue or care before there is a disaster, such as a flood, fire, tornado, earthquake or hurricane. Do not wait for a disaster to strike, for it may be too late to obtain supplies. United Animal Nations' (UAN) Emergency Animal Rescue Service suggests the following:

- Keep a two-week supply of cat food and water. If you use canned food, buy individual size cans with pop-tops. These can be opened easily and there should be nothing left to refrigerate in case of a power outage. To insure freshness use and replenish supplies every three months.
- Store a small litter box, enough litter for two weeks, plastic bags for disposal and a scoop.
- Invest in some form of identification. (See **PAWS to consider/LOST KITTY**, page 96.)
- Store a harness, leash, and small bowls in a carrier for evacuation during a disaster. The carrier should be large enough for the bowls and litter box, and allow me room to stretch out. Write your name and phone number on the carrier.

- Keep a two-week supply of any on-going medications.
- Have a first aid kit. (Pre-assembled kits are available or you can prepare your own — see First Aid Kits).
- Ask my veterinarian if our city has a disaster plan for pets. If I am injured during a disaster, you need to know where to take me. Keep a copy of my medical records and my veterinarian's name and phone number with the emergency supplies or in the carrier.
- Keep an updated photo of us together in case I become lost or if you are required to leave me behind during a disaster. You should be in the picture to prove ownership. Ask a friend or family member outside our area to keep one of the photos in case our home is destroyed during the disaster.

For more information, visit UAN's website at www.uan.org or call 916-429-2457.

FIRST AID KITS. The following is a list of suggestions for a cat first aid kit. When vacationing with me, pack my first aid kit, my veterinarian's phone number, and a blanket in case I must be restrained due to injury. The products included in your kit can be purchased at hardware stores or pharmacies, or from my veterinarian.

TOOLS

chemical ice pack
water-soluble jelly
non-breakable rectal thermometer
pointed tweezers
magnifying glass
syrup of ipecac
blunt-nosed scissors

penlight flashlight
small needle-nosed pliers
eye dropper
latex gloves
first aid book for cats
Pet First Aid Video (available at the American Red Cross office)

ANTIBACTERIAL AGENTS

povidone iodine solution (for disinfecting wounds)
Neosporin®
3% hydrogen peroxide solution for cleaning dirt and blood from a wound
boric acid solution
feline eyewash (do not use drops intended for humans)

DRESSINGS

non-stick wound pads 2"x2", 3"x3", 4"x4"
2 gauze rolls 1x2" wide for wrapping bandaged wounds
6 gauze pads
cotton-tip swabs
1 adhesive tape roll
(Grannicks' Bitter Apple® can be sprayed on bandages and around wounds to deter me from interfering with the healing process.)

There are several preassembled first aid kits on the market. The authors recommend the following one:

Me"OW" First Aid Kit for Cats. A portion of each sale is donated to the Humane Society of the United States. Call Creative Pet Products (877-269-6911) to order.

**FOOD FOR ILL CATS.** It is imperative that I continue to eat and drink water even when I am ill — unless I am vomiting. Force feeding me when I am nauseous will make me vomit more. When a cat does not eat, its body fat begins to break down in order to provide energy. The liver is overwhelmed by the amount of fat it has to convert. The cat can quickly develop a condition called fatty liver disease which can be life-threatening. Entice me to eat with tasty foods, such as deli meats or baby foods. Warming the food increases the aroma. Place baby food on a tongue depressor or on your finger and let me lick it off. Talk to me and stroke me while offering the food. To give water, insert a water filled eye dropper into a corner of my mouth and squeeze the dropper to release the water. Repeat several times. If I do not start to eat or drink after twenty-four hours, take me to my veterinarian. This is a very serious situation. My veterinarian can prescribe an appetite stimulant or — for serious cases — force feed me or use a feeding tube. I may also need to be re-hydrated.

If I am recovering from surgery and am unable to eat on my own, ask my veterinarian if he sells a pudding-like feline food that can be fed to me with a syringe,

**HEIMLICH MANEUVER.** The method used is similar to the one used for humans. Pick up the cat with your hands on its belly below the forelegs and over the rib cage. Hold the cat, facing away from you, and using the heels of both hands, press upward in a quick, jerking motion. It may take several attempts to dislodge an object.

**HYPOTHERMIA OR HYPERTHERMIA.** The symptoms of hypothermia include uncontrollable shivering, decreased respiration and heart rate and disorientation. Frostbite may also occur resulting in the loss of a limb. It is important to <u>raise</u> my body temperature immediately by wrapping me in a blanket. Apply a heating pad or hot water bottle to the outside of the blanket, taking care not to burn me. The possibility of hypothermia is one more reason why I should be kept indoors. If I do not respond to treatment quickly, take me to an emergency clinic or my veterinarian.

The symptoms of hyperthermia include panting and salivating, glazed eyes, rapid heartbeat, warm dry skin, vomiting, unsteadiness and muscle weakness, fatigue or collapse. When these symptoms occur, it is important to <u>lower</u> my body temperature immediately. Remove me from the source of heat and either wrap me in a cool — not cold — water-soaked towel, or spray me with cool water. Offer me a drink of water. I am most susceptible to hyperthermia if I am very young or old; have a history of cardiovascular or respiratory disorders; am a pug-nosed breed or overweight. Hyperthermia, which may result in brain damage or death, can be avoided by never confining me to a hot stuffy enclosed area. If I do not respond to treatment quickly, take me to an emergency clinic or my veterinarian.

**LIQUA SHIELD™.** Liqua Shield™ from Wear Dated® Carpet has a permanent polyethylene barrier built into the backing. This barrier keeps pet accidents from penetrating into the padding and, therefore, prevents mildew and odors.

**PET PREFERENCE™.** This odor eliminator is all natural, non-toxic, and biodegradable. It does a remarkable job of removing pet odors from the home. For more information , call Eco-Aromatic Systems, Inc. at 800-326-1126.

**POISONOUS PLANTS.** Listed below are plants that according to the ASPCA Animal Poison Control Center can kill a cat or make it sick. Remove these plants from my area.

Alfalfa (multiple exposures)
Aloe Vera (Medicine Plant)
Amaryllis
Apple (seeds)
Apple Leaf Croton
Apricot (pit)
Asparagus Fern
Autumn Crocus
Avocado (fruit and pit)
Azalea
Baby's Breath
Bird of Paradise
Bittersweet
Branching Ivy
Buckeye
Buddhist Pine
Caladium
Calla Lily
Castor Bean
Ceriman
Charming Dieffenbachia
Cherry (wilting leaves and seeds)
Chinese Evergreen
Christmas Rose
Cineraria
Clematis
Cordatum
Corn Plant
Croton
Cuban Laurel
Cut Leaf Philodendron
Cycads
Cyclamen
Daffodil
Devil's Ivy
Dieffenbachia (all varieties; commonly called Dumb Cane)
Dracaena Palm

Dragon Tree
Easter Lily
Elaine
Elephant Ears
Emerald Feather
English Ivy
Fiddle-leaf Fig
Florida Beauty
Foxglove
Fruit Salad Plant
Geranium
German Ivy
Giant Dumb Cane
Glacier Ivy
Gold Dieffenbachia
Gold Dust Dracaena
Golden Pothos
Hahn's Self-Branching Ivy
Heartland Philodendron
Hurricane Plant
Indian Rubber Plant
Janet Craig Dracaena
Japanese Show Lily
Jerusalem Cherry
Kalanchoe
Lacy Tree Philodendron
Lily of the Valley
Madagascar Dragon Tree
Marble Queen
Marijuana
Mexican Breadfruit
Miniature Croton (and other varieties)
Mistletoe
Morning Glory
Mother-in-law's Tongue
Narcissus
Needlepoint Ivy

Nephthytis
Nightshade (Solanum species)
Onion
Orleander
Oriental Lily
Peace Lily
Peach (wilting leaves and pit)
Pencil Cactus
Plumosa Fern
Poinsettia (low toxicity)
Poison Ivy and Oak
Pothos (all varieties)
Potato Plant
Precatory Bean
Primrose
Red Emerald
Red Princess
Red-Margined Dracaena
Rhododendron
Ribbon Plant
Saddle Leaf Philodendron
Sago Palm (Cycas)
Satin Pothos
Schefflera
Silver Pothos
Spotted Dumb Cane
String of Pearls/Beads
Striped Dracaena
Sweetheart Ivy
Swiss Cheese Plant
Taro Vine
Tiger Lily
Tomato Plant (green fruit, stem, and leaves)
Tree Philodendron
Tropic Snow Dieffenbachia
Weeping Fig
Yew

*\* Please note: This list is not all inclusive.*

The ASPCA Animal Poison Control Center, an operating division of the American Society for the Prevention of Cruelty to Animals, is the only animal-oriented poison control center in North America. For more information, contact the poisonous plant guide web site at www.napcc.aspca.org. If you are not able to reach my veterinarian in an emergency, call the Animal Poison Control Center, 1-888-426-4435. The Center is open 24 hours a day, seven days a week and charges $45.00 per case. They accept credit cards.

# SPECIAL NOTES ABOUT MY HEALTH CARE

_____

_____

_____

_____

_____

_____

_____

_____

_____

_____

_____

_____

_____

_____

_____

_____

_____

_____

_____

_____

_____

_____

_____

_____

_____

# MY HEALTH CARE RECORD

**INOCULATIONS/TESTS**
(Place a check mark to indicate inoculations and tests have been given.)

DATE GIVEN        ___  ___  ___  ___  ___  ___  ___  ___  ___

LEUKEMIA          ___  ___  ___  ___  ___  ___  ___  ___  ___

RHINOTRACHEITIS   ___  ___  ___  ___  ___  ___  ___  ___  ___

CALICIVIRUS       ___  ___  ___  ___  ___  ___  ___  ___  ___

DISTEMPER         ___  ___  ___  ___  ___  ___  ___  ___  ___

CHLAMYDIA         ___  ___  ___  ___  ___  ___  ___  ___  ___

RABIES            ___  ___  ___  ___  ___  ___  ___  ___  ___

INFECTIOUS
PERITONITIS       ___  ___  ___  ___  ___  ___  ___  ___  ___

WORMING           ___  ___  ___  ___  ___  ___  ___  ___  ___

NOTES             _____

                  _____

                  _____

                  _____

# MY HEALTH CARE RECORD

**INOCULATIONS/TESTS**
(Place a check mark to indicate inoculations and tests have been given.)

DATE GIVEN    ___  ___  ___  ___  ___  ___  ___  ___  ___

LEUKEMIA    ___  ___  ___  ___  ___  ___  ___  ___  ___

RHINOTRACHEITIS    ___  ___  ___  ___  ___  ___  ___  ___

CALICIVIRUS    ___  ___  ___  ___  ___  ___  ___  ___

DISTEMPER    ___  ___  ___  ___  ___  ___  ___  ___  ___

CHLAMYDIA    ___  ___  ___  ___  ___  ___  ___  ___

RABIES    ___  ___  ___  ___  ___  ___  ___  ___

INFECTIOUS
PERITONITIS    ___  ___  ___  ___  ___  ___  ___  ___

WORMING    ___  ___  ___  ___  ___  ___  ___  ___  ___

NOTES    _____

_____

_____

_____

# MY HEALTH CARE RECORD

## ILLNESSES OR INJURIES

Date: _____

Treatment: _____

Home Care Instructions: _____

_____

_____

Date: _____

Treatment: _____

Home Care Instructions: _____

_____

_____

Date: _____

Treatment: _____

Home Care Instructions: _____

_____

_____

Date: _____

Treatment: _____

Home Care Instructions: _____

_____

_____

Date: _____

Treatment: _____

Home Care Instructions: _____

_____

_____

# MY HEALTH CARE RECORD

## ILLNESSES OR INJURIES

Date: _____

Treatment: _____

Home Care Instructions: _____

_____

_____


Date: _____

Treatment: _____

Home Care Instructions: _____

_____

_____


Date: _____

Treatment: _____

Home Care Instructions: _____

_____

_____


Date: _____

Treatment: _____

Home Care Instructions: _____

_____

_____


Date: _____

Treatment: _____

Home Care Instructions: _____

_____

_____

# PAWS to consider

DYING. Because my expected life span is usually ten to eighteen years, it is unlikely that I will outlive you. You may, therefore, have to face the unpleasant thought of having me euthanized. Euthanasia is very difficult for both you and me, but is an event that must be faced. If I am ill, suffering, or have poor quality of life, do not wait too long to euthanize me.

I would like to offer the following suggestions when the time comes to say "Goodbye." Upon taking me to the veterinarian, it is best if you stay with me. It will be comforting to me, even though it may be hard for you. Hold me in your arms while the veterinarian sedates me. After I am asleep, the veterinarian will inject me with a pentobarbital solution. This method keeps me from suffering and makes the whole process easier. Some veterinarians will come to our home or to our car for the euthanasia process. If the veterinarian's office has always made me nervous, this is a good option.

Children should be told what is going to happen to me. If they are teenagers, they may want to be present when I am euthanized. Be sure that the children understand the meaning of the words "put down," "put to sleep," or "euthanized". The words "put to sleep" may be confusing and frightening to a small child. Let the children know that they are not the cause of my leaving and validate their feelings of sadness. Encourage discussion about my death.

If there are other cats and dogs in the household, comfort them for they may also grieve my absence. If possible, allow them to view my body which may ease their anxiety and help them accept the finality of my departure.

After my death, take care of my body in one of the following ways.

1. My veterinarian can dispose of my body in a communal cremation. If you wish a private cremation, an urn or box for my remains can be ordered through my veterinarian or a pet cemeterian.
2. You can take me home and bury my body if your city's regulations allow it. Use a box or purchase an air-tight pet casket through my veterinarian. Usually a casket can be unearthed and moved if you relocate and wish to rebury my body at the new location. When burying my body, leave two feet of compacted soil above my box or casket which will keep other animals from digging up my remains.
3. You can take me to a pet cemetery. Pet cemetery staff can provide understanding support. For information about pet cemeteries or crematories contact:

International Association of Pet Cemeteries
1-800-952-5541

Grieving after I die is completely normal and natural. Whether I have been your pet for a short time or for many years, I have been a valued member of your family. I will be sadly missed. At this time it is important to have friends and family near who understand and are sensitive to the grief you may be feeling. Do not expect everyone to know how saddened you are by my loss. Well-meaning friends, who have never owned a cat, might try to cheer you up by remarking that, "It was only a cat!" Do not be offended when they do not understand. Your feelings are valid. If you have problems coping, ask my veterinarian about a pet loss support group in your area. There are several pet grief hotlines throughout the country. The Rhode Island Veterinary Medical Association lists the following:

    530-752-4200 — Staffed by University of California-Davis veterinary students
    630-603-3994 — Staffed by Chicago VMA veterinarians and staff
    607-253-3932 — Staffed by Cornell University veterinary students
    217-244-2273 — Staffed by University of Illinois veterinary students
    888-478-7574 — Staffed by Iowa State University veterinary students and
                   community volunteers
    517-432-2696 — Staffed by Michigan State University veterinary students
    614-292-1823 — Staffed by Ohio State University veterinary students
    508-839-7966 — Staffed by Tufts University veterinary students
    540-231-8038 — Staffed by Virginia-Maryland Regional College of Veterinary
                   Medicine

The American Veterinary Medical Association (AVMA) has published two brochures called "Pet Loss: How Do I Know When It Is Time" and "When Your Animal Dies: Understanding Your Feeling of Loss." They are free and can be obtained by writing AVMA, 1931 N. Meacham Road, Suite 100, Schaumburg, Illinois 60173. The Chicago Veterinary Medical Association (CVMA) has published a brochure called "Losing a Special Companion: Resolving the Grief, Remembering the Good." The brochure is free and can be secured by writing to the CVMA, 120 East Ogden Avenue, Suite 17C, Hinsdale, Illinois 60521.

You need time to work through your grief before bringing another pet home. Although a new pet will not take my place, it will have its own unique personality and bring you as much happiness as I have. It is usually not a good idea to get a look-alike pet because you may tend to compare it to me.

(There is not much that we, the authors, can offer to make your cat's death easier except the knowledge, that through the passage of time, the pain is replaced with warm memories. We know, because we have walked this path before. In fact, even with the passage of time, it was difficult for us to write this section. It is a heartbreaking time, but hopefully, the stories and photos you have preserved in this book will bring you fond memories.)

Another factor that should be considered is the possibility that you may die before me. Making arrangements in your will can insure that I will be properly cared for. Before listing a caregiver's name in your will, be sure the person has agreed to be responsible for me after your death. List a second person as a backup if your first choice cannot assume the responsibility of my care. By law you are not allowed to leave money to me because I am considered property. The money for my care can be established in a pet trust which is similar to a trust for humans. A trustee is designated to manage the trust for my benefit. The trust can detail an amount to be spent monthly or annually for my care. If I have a companion pet, request that we are not to be separated, except for medical reasons. Arrange to donate the balance of the trust to your favorite charity after my death.

If you do not have a caregiver to list in your will, there are "retirement" homes for cats located throughout the United states. There is a fee for a "retirement" home because the facility you choose will care for me for the rest of my life. If possible, visit various facilities before making a decision about my care. The facility you choose should provide me with love, food, water, grooming and visits to a veterinarian for yearly check-ups, dental cleaning and vaccinations. When you have selected a "retirement" home, the staff will provide you with a pet care registration and bequest form. List my special needs on the form. A copy of my medical history will be required. I will be disqualified from some programs if I have feline leukemia or behavioral problems toward humans.

Listed below are four "retirement" homes. Check the internet for more listings.

> The Bluebell Foundation for Cats, (949) 494-1586, 20982 Laguna Canyon Road, Laguna Beach, California, or visit www.bluebell.org
> Cat Care Society, (303) 239-9690, 5985 W. 11th Ave., Lakewood, Colorado 80214, or visit www.catcaresociety.org
> The Hermitage No-Kill Cat Shelter, (520) 571-7839, P.O. Box 13508, Tucson, AR 85732, or visit www.scottnet. com/cats
> The Wild Cat Ranch Pet Retirement Center, (830) 995-4689, 137 Upper Sisterdale Road, Comfort, TX 78013, or visit www.wildcatranch.net.

The North Shore Animal League in Port Washington, New York, has a "Surviving Pet Care" program. They cannot house me, but will find a loving home for me after you die. Their phone number is 516-883-7682. After I am placed, North Shore conducts semi-annual visits to my adoptive home to insure that I am happy, healthy and loved. There is a fee for these services. Your local no-kill shelter may have a similar program.

The facility you choose and the monetary requirement should be listed in your will. A copy of the forms concerning my care should be attached to the will. Update my medical history as needed. If you die before me, it is comforting to know that I will be cared for. After your death, I may grieve your absence, but with love and proper care, I will eventually adjust to my new home.

# INDEX

# ABOUT THE AUTHOR AND HER CAT

**DALE AND KATHY**
(Photograph by Dave Beatty Studio
Springfield, Illinois)

Kathy Kinser delights in creating humerous poetry for parties, travel and other special events. Her poems have chronicled travel experiences on all seven continents with husband, Dave, a retired Springfield, Illinois ophthalmologist. The Kinsers enjoy seeking out and riding monster roller coasters at amusement parks across the country. Kathy maintains active memberships in the P.E.O. Sisterhood and the Illinois Symphony Guild of Springfield.

In the spring of 1993 an emaciated black tomcat appeared on the Kinser patio and collapsed. He was suffering from internal parasites and wounds sustained as a result of living paw to mouth in the great outdoors. Kathy felt that adoption seemed to be the only humane plan of action. After several veterinary visits, a radical change of diet and months of recovery, Dale, 'The Cat', was transformed into a playful fourteen pound feline with bright eyes and a luxurious coat. Dale employs his relaxed personality as one of several office cats that welcome feline and canine patients at Springfield's West Lake Animal Hospital.

Dale's canine companion in the Kinser home was Chocolate Chip, a chocolate Labrador, until Chip's untimely death from cancer in 1998. Shortly after losing Chip, Kathy received an urgent call from a friend who was keeping an abandoned two month old puppy. She asked Kathy if she and Dave would give it a temporary home. The puppy quickly won their hearts and temporary is now long term! Kathy named the puppy Symphony Sunday in honor of the day he was acquired. He has developed into an intelligent dog who knows he is very special.

# ABOUT THE AUTHOR AND HER CAT

Miss Florida, one of the inspirations for this book, didn't always live a cushy life in Springfield, Illinois. During her first year, she was one of forty strays at a resort in Orlando, Florida. While Jodi Alessandrini and her husband, Joe, were visiting that resort, they put food out each day for the stray cats. Since none of the other cats staked a claim on Jodi, Miss Florida decided to put her best paw forward. She batted her lovely green eyes and purred in Jodi's ear. She even jumped into Jodi's suitcase while Jodi was preparing to leave. However, her plan went awry when Jodi left without her. Miss Florida heard the words — ticket, veterinarian and shots but didn't have the slightest idea what any of them meant. Furthermore, it appeared that the humans did not understand "felinese" since Miss Florida thought she had been sending a very clear message.

**MISS FLORI AND JODI**
(Photograph by Studio 131
Springfield, Illinois)

Three weeks went by. Colored lights and decorations were put on trees and some snow even fell in Florida. Only Miss Florida and one other cat were left at the resort so they stayed together and somehow avoided the Animal Control people. Just when it may have seemed all was lost to Miss Florida, she heard a voice from the past. She and Jodi were reunited and the other kitty was taken to a no-kill shelter and later adopted. After a two day delay in the Orlando airport, Miss Florida boarded a plane with Jodi and flew to Illinois. It took three months to bring Miss Flori to her proper weight, rid her of parasites and mend the wound in her tail. As one can see from the picture, she has blossomed into a very majestic cat with lovely green eyes, a luxurious coat and a very long, fluffy tail. She has a sweet and playful disposition. Jodi is honored to have been selected for adoption by such an outstanding cat.

Besides Miss Flori, Jodi and her husband share their home with two dogs — an American Eskimo breed, named Palla di Neve, (Nevi), which means ball of snow in Italian, and a golden retriever mix named Katie. Jodi and her husband are the parents of two married daughters and "grandparents" to five cats and one dog. Jodi owns and operates a talent agency and writes and produces murder mystery events. She is a member of Women in Management, the P.E.O. Sisterhood and the Illinois Symphony Guild of Springfield. She volunteers on behalf of the local Animal Protective League and has chaired several fundraisers for them. Her work with stray animals, and the creative antics of Miss Flori, prompted her to co-author this book. She is also the co-author of Puppy Stuff.

128

# NOTABLE NUMBERS AND ADDRESSES

**My Veterinarian**

Name: _____

Address: _____

Phone: _____

**24 Hour Emergency Pet Clinic**

Address: _____

Phone: _____

**Poison Control Center**

Phone: _____

**My Pet Sitter**

Name: _____

Address: _____

Phone: _____

**My Kennel**

Name: _____

Address: _____

Phone: _____

**My Groomer**

Name: _____

Address: _____

Phone: _____

**My Insurance Company**

Phone: _____

**Animal Shelter**

Phone: _____

**Newspaper Classified (Lost Pet Service)**

Phone: _____

# CAT SITTER INSTRUCTIONS FOR THE CARE OF

_____
(MY NAME)

from _____ to _____
       (DATE)              (DATE)

My veterinarian's name is _____

Veterinarian's phone number: _____

Veterinarian's address: _____

Emergency veterinary phone number: _____

My form of identification is _____ My ID # is _____

My owner will be at: _____

My owner can be reached at this phone number, _____

or my owner wishes you to call _____
                                              (NAME)

at _____ if I have any problems.
        (PHONE NUMBER)

Location of my supplies:

    Food and water bowls _____

    Food and treats _____

    Daily medications _____

    Toys _____

    Grooming tools _____

    First-aid kit _____

    Litter box and supplies _____

    Bed _____

    Medical records _____

Instructions:

    Feeding _____

    Exercise _____

    Grooming _____

# CAT SITTER INSTRUCTIONS FOR THE CARE OF

_____
(MY NAME)

from _____ to _____
        (DATE)        (DATE)

My veterinarian's name is _____

Veterinarian's phone number: _____

Veterinarian's address: _____

Emergency veterinary phone number: _____

My form of identification is _____ My ID # is _____

My owner will be at: _____

My owner can be reached at this phone number, _____

or my owner wishes you to call _____
                                   (NAME)

at _____ if I have any problems.
      (PHONE NUMBER)

Location of my supplies:

    Food and water bowls _____

    Food and treats _____

    Daily medications _____

    Toys _____

    Grooming tools _____

    First-aid kit _____

    Litter box and supplies _____

    Bed _____

    Medical records _____

Instructions:

    Feeding _____

    Exercise _____

    Grooming _____

## CAT SITTER INSTRUCTIONS FOR THE CARE OF

_____
(MY NAME)

from _____ to _____
     (DATE)           (DATE)

My veterinarian's name is _____

Veterinarian's phone number: _____

Veterinarian's address: _____

Emergency veterinary phone number: _____

My form of identification is _____ My ID # is _____

My owner will be at: _____

My owner can be reached at this phone number, _____

or my owner wishes you to call _____
                                      (NAME)

at _____ if I have any problems.
     (PHONE NUMBER)

Location of my supplies:

    Food and water bowls _____

    Food and treats _____

    Daily medications _____

    Toys _____

    Grooming tools _____

    First-aid kit _____

    Litter box and supplies _____

    Bed _____

    Medical records _____

Instructions:

    Feeding _____

    Exercise _____

    Grooming _____

## CAT SITTER INSTRUCTIONS FOR THE CARE OF

_____

(MY NAME)

from —————————— to ——————————
      (DATE)           (DATE)

My veterinarian's name is _____

Veterinarian's phone number: _____

Veterinarian's address: _____

Emergency veterinary phone number: _____

My form of identification is _____ My ID # is _____

My owner will be at: _____

My owner can be reached at this phone number, _____

or my owner wishes you to call _____
                                         (NAME)

at _____ if I have any problems.
   (PHONE NUMBER)

Location of my supplies:

    Food and water bowls _____

    Food and treats _____

    Daily medications _____

    Toys _____

    Grooming tools _____

    First-aid kit _____

    Litter box and supplies _____

    Bed _____

    Medical records _____

Instructions:

    Feeding _____

    Exercise _____

    Grooming _____

# CAT SITTER INSTRUCTIONS FOR THE CARE OF

_____

(MY NAME)

from _____ to _____

(DATE)                    (DATE)

My veterinarian's name is _____

Veterinarian's phone number: _____

Veterinarian's address: _____

Emergency veterinary phone number: _____

My form of identification is _____ My ID # is _____

My owner will be at: _____

My owner can be reached at this phone number, _____

or my owner wishes you to call _____

(NAME)

at _____ if I have any problems.

(PHONE NUMBER)

Location of my supplies:

    Food and water bowls _____

    Food and treats _____

    Daily medications _____

    Toys _____

    Grooming tools _____

    First-aid kit _____

    Litter box and supplies _____ _____

    Bed _____

    Medical records _____

Instructions:

    Feeding _____

    Exercise _____

    Grooming _____

# CAT SITTER INSTRUCTIONS FOR THE CARE OF

_____
(MY NAME)

from —————————— to ——————————
(DATE)                        (DATE)

My veterinarian's name is _____

Veterinarian's phone number: _____

Veterinarian's address: _____

Emergency veterinary phone number: _____

My form of identification is _____ My ID # is _____

My owner will be at: _____

My owner can be reached at this phone number, _____

or my owner wishes you to call _____
(NAME)

at _____ if I have any problems.
(PHONE NUMBER)

Location of my supplies:

    Food and water bowls _____

    Food and treats _____

    Daily medications _____

    Toys _____

    Grooming tools _____

    First-aid kit _____

    Litter box and supplies _____

    Bed _____

    Medical records _____

Instructions:

    Feeding _____

    Exercise _____

    Grooming _____

## CAT SITTER INSTRUCTIONS FOR THE CARE OF

_____
(MY NAME)

from _____ to _____
          (DATE)                    (DATE)

My veterinarian's name is _____

Veterinarian's phone number: _____

Veterinarian's address: _____

Emergency veterinary phone number: _____

My form of identification is _____ My ID # is _____

My owner will be at: _____

My owner can be reached at this phone number, _____

or my owner wishes you to call _____
                                                          (NAME)

at _____ if I have any problems.
        (PHONE NUMBER)

Location of my supplies:

    Food and water bowls _____

    Food and treats _____

    Daily medications _____

    Toys _____

    Grooming tools _____

    First-aid kit _____

    Litter box and supplies _____

    Bed _____

    Medical records _____

Instructions:

    Feeding _____

    Exercise _____

    Grooming _____

# CAT SITTER INSTRUCTIONS FOR THE CARE OF

_____
(MY NAME)

from _____ to _____
      (DATE)        (DATE)

My veterinarian's name is _____

Veterinarian's phone number: _____

Veterinarian's address: _____

Emergency veterinary phone number: _____

My form of identification is _____ My ID # is _____

My owner will be at: _____

My owner can be reached at this phone number, _____

or my owner wishes you to call _____
                                          (NAME)

at _____ if I have any problems.
   (PHONE NUMBER)

Location of my supplies:

    Food and water bowls _____

    Food and treats _____

    Daily medications _____

    Toys _____

    Grooming tools _____

    First-aid kit _____

    Litter box and supplies _____

    Bed _____

    Medical records _____

Instructions:

    Feeding _____

    Exercise _____

    Grooming _____

## CAT KENNEL INSTRUCTIONS FOR THE CARE OF

_____
(MY NAME)

from _____ to _____
          (DATE)                    (DATE)

My veterinarian's name is _____

Veterinarian's phone number: _____

Veterinarian's address: _____

Emergency veterinary phone number: _____

My form of identification is _____ My ID # is _____

My owner will be at: _____

My owner can be reached at this phone number, _____

or my owner wishes you to call _____
                                                                      (NAME)

at _____ if I have any problems.
          (PHONE NUMBER)

Special instructions: _____

_____

_____

I am bringing the following toys and supplies: _____

_____

## CAT KENNEL INSTRUCTIONS FOR THE CARE OF

_____
(MY NAME)

from _____ to _____
          (DATE)                    (DATE)

My veterinarian's name is _____

Veterinarian's phone number: _____

Veterinarian's address: _____

Emergency veterinary phone number: _____

My form of identification is _____ My ID # is _____

My owner will be at: _____

My owner can be reached at this phone number, _____

or my owner wishes you to call _____
                                                                      (NAME)

at _____ if I have any problems.
          (PHONE NUMBER)

Special instructions: _____

_____

_____

I am bringing the following toys and supplies: _____

_____

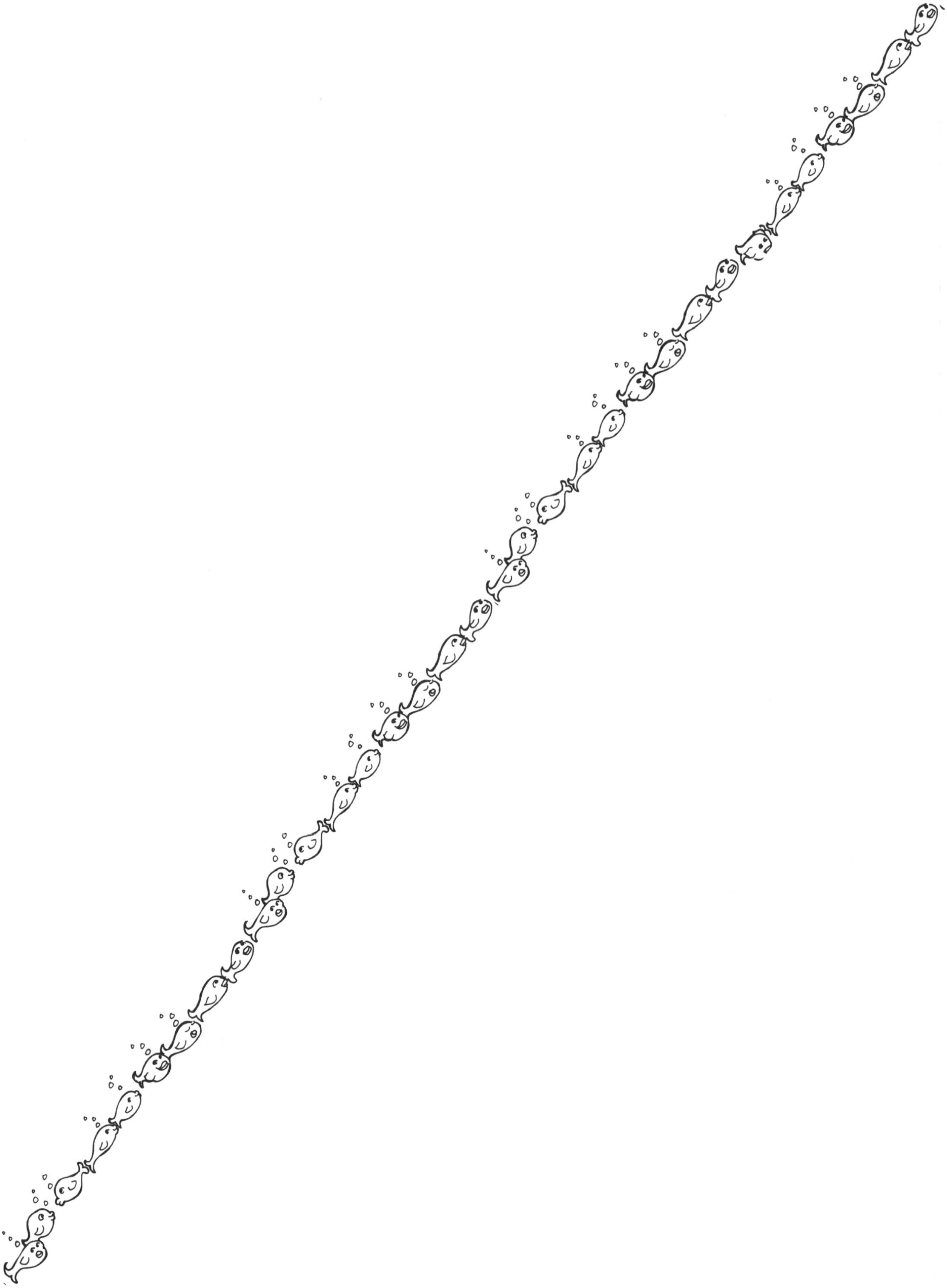

## CAT KENNEL INSTRUCTIONS FOR THE CARE OF

_____
(MY NAME)

from _____ to _____
          (DATE)              (DATE)

My veterinarian's name is _____

Veterinarian's phone number: _____

Veterinarian's address:_____

Emergency veterinary phone number: _____

My form of identification is _____ My ID # is _____

My owner will be at: _____

My owner can be reached at this phone number, _____

or my owner wishes you to call _____
                                                              (NAME)

at _____ if I have any problems.
          (PHONE NUMBER)

Special instructions: _____

_____

_____

I am bringing the following toys and supplies: _____

_____

- - - - - - - - - - - - - - - - - - - - - - - - - - - - - - - - - - - - - - - - - - - - - -

## CAT KENNEL INSTRUCTIONS FOR THE CARE OF

_____
(MY NAME)

from _____ to _____
          (DATE)              (DATE)

My veterinarian's name is _____

Veterinarian's phone number: _____

Veterinarian's address:_____

Emergency veterinary phone number: _____

My form of identification is _____ My ID # is _____

My owner will be at: _____

My owner can be reached at this phone number, _____

or my owner wishes you to call _____
                                                              (NAME)

at _____ if I have any problems.
          (PHONE NUMBER)

Special instructions: _____

_____

_____

I am bringing the following toys and supplies: _____

_____

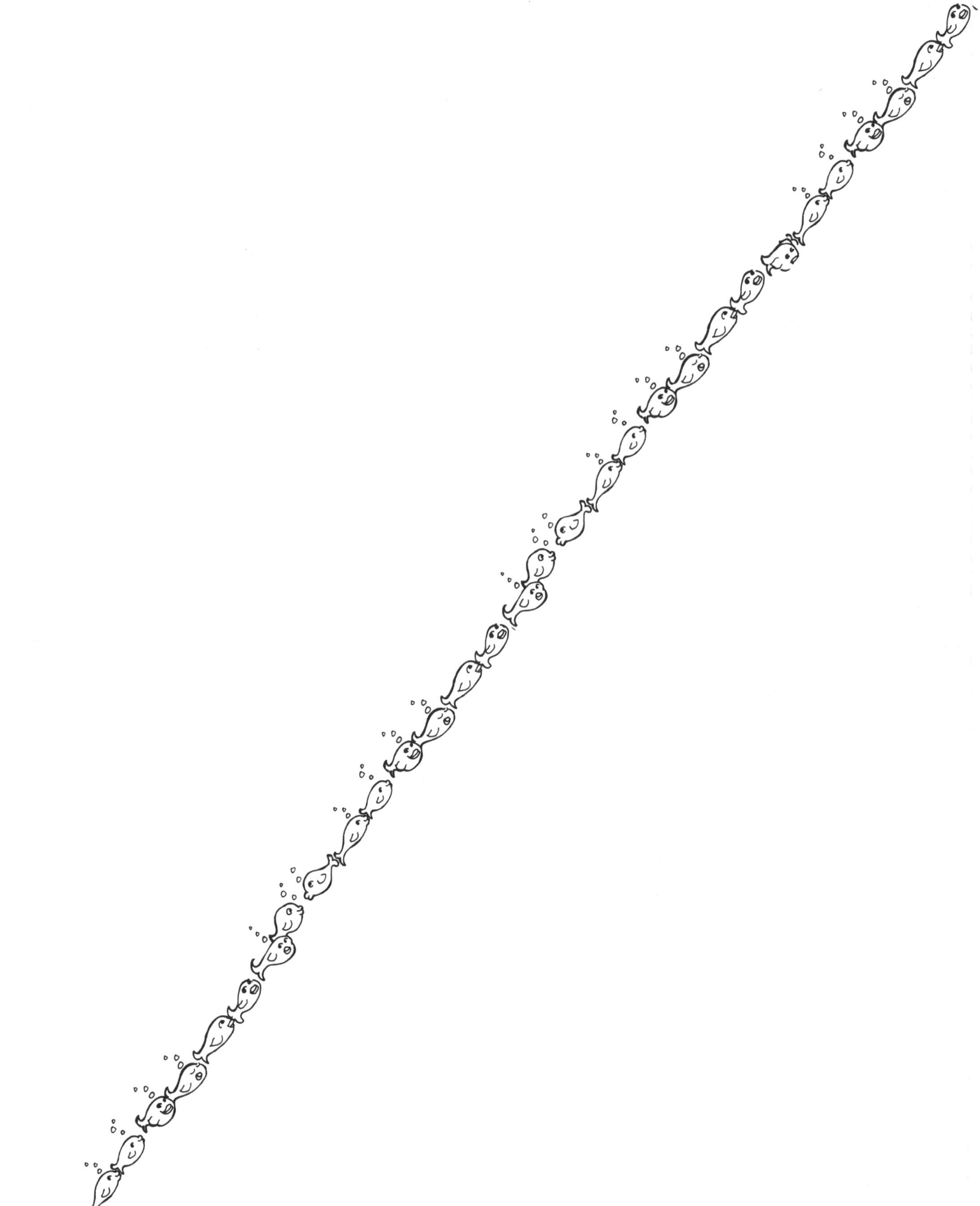

## CAT KENNEL INSTRUCTIONS FOR THE CARE OF

_____
(MY NAME)

from _____ to _____
      (DATE)           (DATE)

My veterinarian's name is _____

Veterinarian's phone number: _____

Veterinarian's address:_____

Emergency veterinary phone number: _____

My form of identification is _____ My ID # is _____

My owner will be at: _____

My owner can be reached at this phone number, _____

or my owner wishes you to call _____
                                      (NAME)

at _____ if I have any problems.
     (PHONE NUMBER)

Special instructions: _____

_____

_____

I am bringing the following toys and supplies: _____

_____

- - - - - - - - - - - - - - - - - - - - - - - - - - - - - - - -

## CAT KENNEL INSTRUCTIONS FOR THE CARE OF

_____
(MY NAME)

from _____ to _____
      (DATE)             (DATE)

My veterinarian's name is _____

Veterinarian's phone number: _____

Veterinarian's address:_____

Emergency veterinary phone number: _____

My form of identification is _____ My ID # is _____

My owner will be at: _____

My owner can be reached at this phone number, _____

or my owner wishes you to call _____
                                        (NAME)

at _____ if I have any problems.
     (PHONE NUMBER)

Special instructions: _____

_____

_____

I am bringing the following toys and supplies: _____

_____

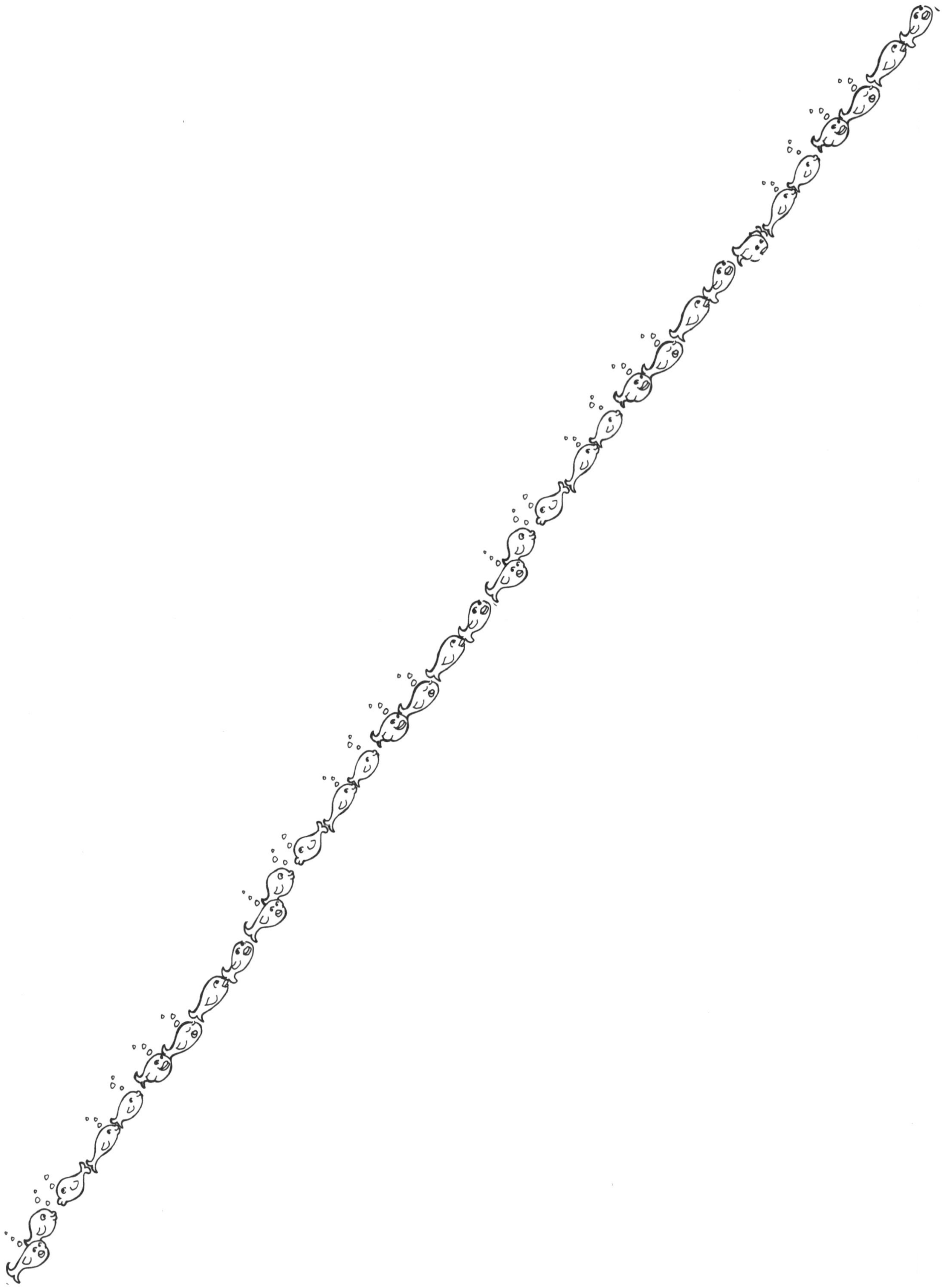

## ORDER FORM

If <u>KITTY STUFF</u> or <u>PUPPY STUFF</u> is not available in your local book store, additional copies can be ordered by sending a check or money order payable to PALLACHIP PUBLISHING and this completed form to:  PALLACHIP PUBLISHING, 37 OAKMONT DRIVE, SPRING-FIELD, IL  62704.  The price per book is $ ____24.95____ .

YOUR NAME _____
(PLEASE PRINT)

ADDRESS _____
(no deliveries to P.O. Boxes or outside the continental U.S.)

_____

CITY/ZIP/STATE _____

DAYTIME PHONE (_____) _____

I am ordering _____ <u>KITTY STUFF</u> _____ <u>PUPPY STUFF</u> (Please check)

Please send _____ copies   @  $ __24.95__ each                              $_____

Illinois residents add                    $ __1.80__ Sales tax per book       $_____

Shipping and handling          @ $ __3.50__ per book                           $_____

Total order                                                                                      $_____
Allow two (2) weeks for delivery.

---

## ORDER FORM

If <u>KITTY STUFF</u> or <u>PUPPY STUFF</u> is not available in your local book store, additional copies can be ordered by sending a check or money order payable to PALLACHIP PUBLISHING and this completed form to:  PALLACHIP PUBLISHING, 37 OAKMONT DRIVE, SPRING-FIELD, IL  62704.  The price per book is $ ____24.95____ .

YOUR NAME _____
(PLEASE PRINT)

ADDRESS _____
(no deliveries to P.O. Boxes or outside the continental U.S.)

_____

CITY/ZIP/STATE _____

DAYTIME PHONE (_____) _____

I am ordering _____ <u>KITTY STUFF</u> _____ <u>PUPPY STUFF</u> (Please check)

Please send _____ copies   @  $ __24.95__ each                              $_____

Illinois residents add                    $ __1.80__ Sales tax per book       $_____

Shipping and handling          @ $ __3.50__ per book                           $_____

Total order                                                                                      $_____
Allow two (2) weeks for delivery.

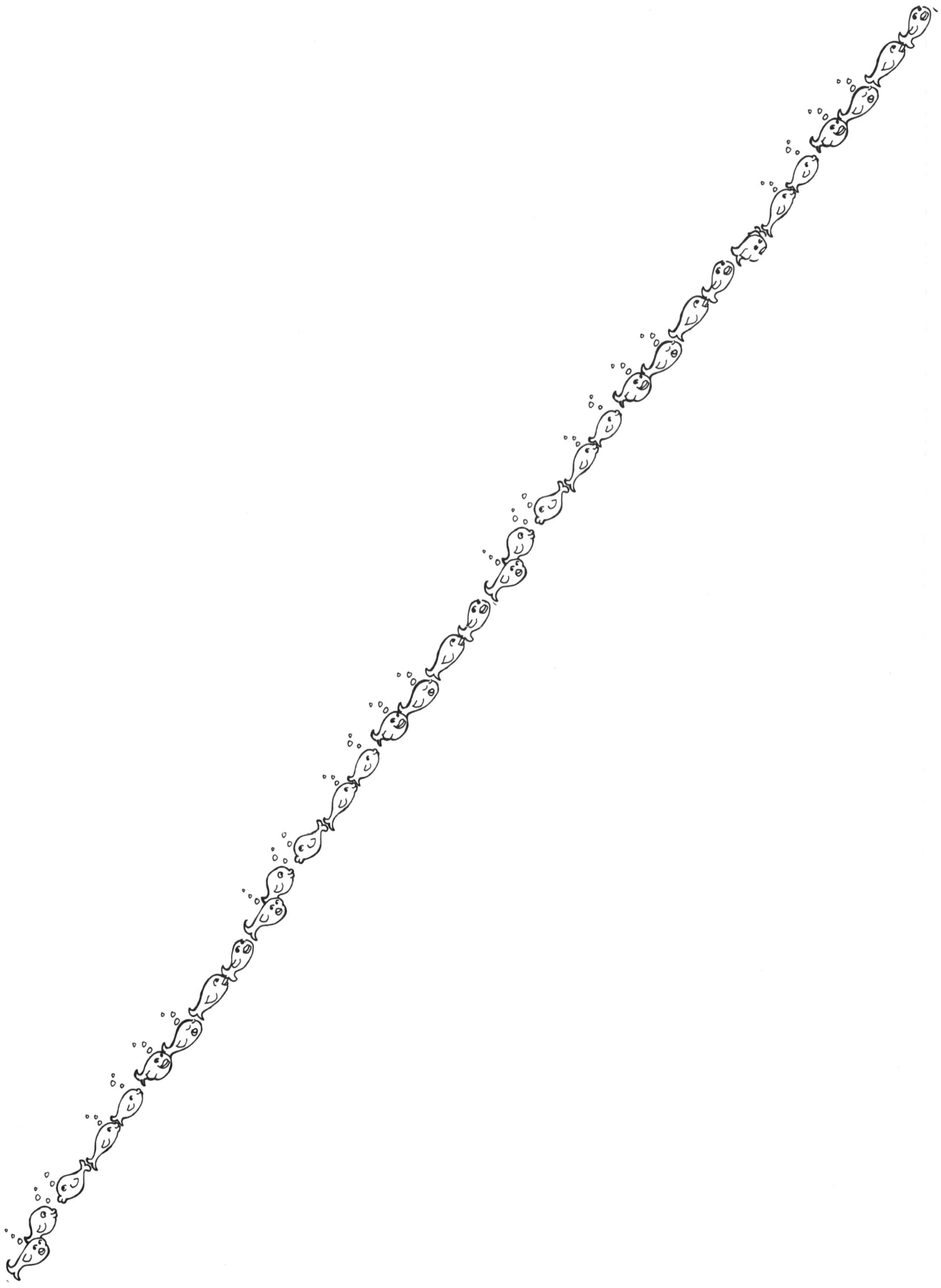